THE ANDALUCÍAN COAST TO COAST WALK

About the Author

Guy Hunter-Watts has lived and worked in Andalucía since the 1980s. After studying at the universities of Santiago and Salamanca he taught English in South America before moving to the Ronda mountains where he's been leading guided walks for almost 30 years. His work as a guide and freelance journalist has taken him to many corners of the planet including India, Namibia, Tanzania, Mexico, Peru and Mongolia.

Other Cicerone guides by the author
Walking in Andalucía
Coastal Walks in Andalucía
The Mountains of Ronda & Grazalema

THE ANDALUCÍAN COAST TO COAST WALK

FROM THE MEDITERRANEAN TO THE ATLANTIC THROUGH THE BAETIC MOUNTAINS

by Guy Hunter-Watts

JUNIPER HOUSE, MURLEY MOSS,
OXENHOLME ROAD, KENDAL, CUMBRIA LA9 7RL
www.cicerone.co.uk

Printed in China on behalf of Latitude Press Ltd
A catalogue record for this book is available from the British Library.
All photographs are by the author unless otherwise stated.

Route mapping by Lovell Johns www.lovelljohns.com
Contains OpenStreetMap.org data © OpenStreetMap
contributors, CC-BY-SA. NASA relief data courtesy of ESRI

With thanks to A. W. for providing the initial inspiration and to all those who joined me on the walk when raising funds for Nepal.

Updates to this Guide

While every effort is made by our authors to ensure the accuracy of guidebooks as they go to print, changes can occur during the lifetime of an edition. Any updates that we know of for this guide will be on the Cicerone website (www.cicerone.co.uk/970/updates), so please check before planning your trip. We also advise that you check information about such things as transport, accommodation and shops locally. Even rights of way can be altered over time.

The route maps in this guide are derived from publicly available data, databases and crowd-sourced data. As such they have not been through the detailed checking procedures that would generally be applied to a published map from an official mapping agency, although naturally we have reviewed them closely in the light of local knowledge as part of the preparation of this guide.

We are always grateful for information about any discrepancies between a guidebook and the facts on the ground, sent by email to updatesatcicerone.co.uk or by post to Cicerone, Juniper House, Murley Moss, Oxenholme Road, Kendal, LA9 7RL.

Register your book: To sign up to receive free updates, special offers and GPX files where available, register your book at www.cicerone.co.uk.

Front cover: The Sierra de Tejeda, Almijara y Alhama between Maro and Frigliana (Day 1)

CONTENTS

Map key 7
Overview map 8–9
Route summary table 11
Author's preface 13

INTRODUCTION 15
The Andalucían Coast to Coast Walk: an overview 15
Plants and wildlife 20
Andalucía: the historical context 22
Getting there 26
When to go 28
Accommodation. 28
Eating out in southern Spain 29
Language 30
Money 31
Communications 31
What to take. 31
Maps 32
Staying safe 32
Using this guide 33

THE ROUTE 35
Day 1   Maro to Frigiliana 36
Day 2   Frigiliana to Cómpeta 44
Day 3   Cómpeta to Sedella. 52
Day 4   Sedella to Alcaucín 60
Day 5   Alcaucín to Ventas de Zafarraya 68
Day 6   Ventas de Zafarraya to Riogordo 76
Day 7   Riogordo to Villanueva de Cauche 85
Day 8   Villanueva de Cauche to Villanueva de la Concepción 92
Day 9   Villanueva de la Concepción to Valle de Abdalajís 100
Day 10   Valle de Abdalajís to Carratraca via El Chorro 107
Day 11   Carratraca to El Burgo 117
Day 12   El Burgo to Ronda. 125
Day 13   Ronda to Montejaque 134
Day 14   Montejaque to Cortes de la Frontera 142
Day 15   Cortes de la Frontera to El Colmenar 149
Day 16   El Colmenar to Jimena de la Frontera 157

Day 17   Jimena de la Frontera to Castillo de Castellar 168
Day 18   Castillo de Castellar to Los Barrios 176
Day 19   Los Barrios to El Pelayo 185
Day 20   El Pelayo to Tarifa 193
Day 21   Tarifa to Bolonia 202

Appendix A   Useful contacts 209
Appendix B   Glossary 210
Appendix C   Further reading 212

Symbols used on route maps

	route
	alternative route
	footpath
	track
	vehicle track
	tarmac road
(S)	start point
(F)	finish point
	woodland
	urban areas
	station/railway
▲	peak
⋀	campsite
■	building
☗	church
)(	pass
•	water feature
≅	bridge
⟱	picnic area
⊞	cemetery
✺	*mirador* (viewpoint)
•	other feature
⬢	cave

Relief
in metres

2600–2800
2400–2600
2200–2400
2000–2200
1800–2000
1600–1800
1400–1600
1200–1400
1000–1200
800–1000
600–800
400–600
200–400
0–200

Contour lines are drawn at 50m intervals and highlighted at 200m intervals.

SCALE: 1:100,000

0 kilometres 1 2
0 miles 1

GPX files
GPX files for all routes can be downloaded free at www.cicerone.co.uk/970/GPX.

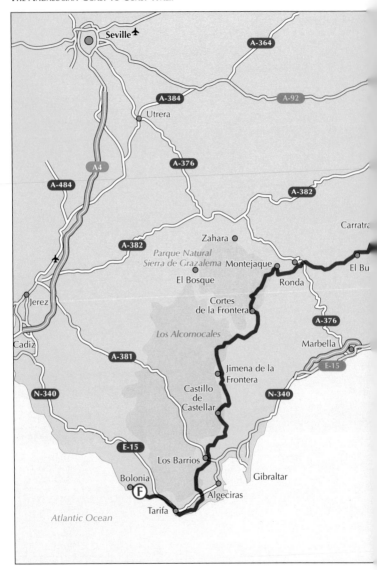

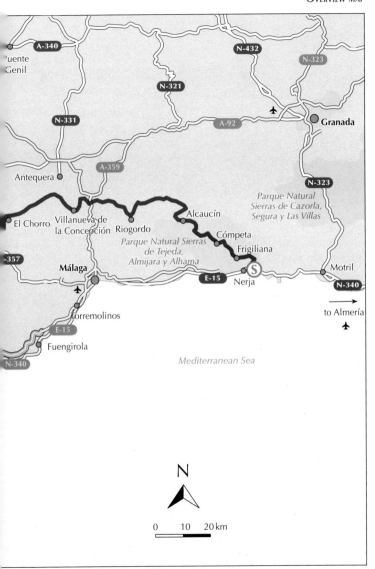

Along the old railway track towards Riogordo (Day 6)

ROUTE SUMMARY TABLE

Stage	Start/finish	Grade	Distance	Ascent/Descent	Time	Page
1	Maro – Frigiliana	Medium/Difficult	15.2km	930m/660m	5hr 35min	36
2	Frigiliana – Cómpeta	Medium/Difficult	18.5km	915m/615m	6hr	44
3	Cómpeta – Sedella	Medium	14km	575m/520m	4hr 30min	52
4	Sedella – Alcaucín	Difficult	17.3km	1050m/860m	6hr 40min	60
5	Alcaucín – Ventas de Zafarraya	Medium/Difficult	18.5km	650m/250m	5hr 30min	68
6	Ventas de Zafarraya – Riogordo	Medium/Difficult	23.4km	345m/865m	6hr 30min	76
7	Riogordo – Villanueva de Cauche	Medium/Difficult	16.3km	710m/410m	4hr 45min	85
8	Villanueva de Cauche – Villanueva de la Concepción	Medium	15km	390m/490m	4hr 30min	92
9	Villanueva de la Concepción – Valle de Abdalajís	Medium/Difficult	21.3km	490m/650m	6hr	100
10	Valle de Abdalajís – Carratraca	Difficult	25.8km	1100m/910m	7hr 30min	107
11	Carratraca – El Burgo	Medium/Difficult	22.8km	785m/750m	6hr 45min	117
12	El Burgo – Ronda	Difficult	26.3km	755m/590m	7hr 15min	125
13	Ronda – Montejaque	Medium	11.7km	410m/450m	3hr 50min	134
14	Montejaque – Cortes de la Frontera	Medium/Difficult	19.5km	635m/705m	6hr	142
15	Cortes de la Frontera – El Colmenar	Medium	15.8km	515m/890m	5hr	149
16	El Colmenar – Jimena de la Frontera	Difficult	25km	670m/815m	7hr	157
17	Jimena de la Frontera – Castillo de Castellar	Medium	22.1km	285m/125m	5hr 40min	168
18	Castillo de Castellar – Los Barrios	Medium/Difficult	24.5m	340m/565m	6hr 45min	176
19	Los Barrios – El Pelayo	Medium/Difficult	25.5km	575m/350m	7hr 5min	185
20	El Pelayo – Tarifa	Medium	17.4km	165m/405m	4hr 55min	193
21	Tarifa – Bolonia	Medium	20.5km	40m/45m	5hr	202
Total	Maro – Bolonia		416.4km	12,330m/11,920m	21 days	

The restored hamlet at El Acebuchal (Day 2)

AUTHOR'S PREFACE

The idea of a long-distance walk through Andalucía linking the Mediterranean Sea and the Atlantic Ocean had long intrigued me and some twenty years ago I began plotting a route across the southern mountains. Life took an unexpected turn and the project lay dormant for almost a decade. But the appeal of charting such a walk never diminished. Inspired by the knowledge that Carthaginians and Phoenicians, Greeks and Romans, Visigoths and Moors had all walked through these same mountains it was also hugely exciting to think that it was along the valleys of southern Iberia that Man first walked out of Africa into Europe. The notion that the walk would be following in the footsteps of so many ancient peoples was both fascinating and humbling.

Thus was born – 10 years ago now – the Coast to Coast Walk, a 21-day adventure which links two seas and six of Andalucía's beautiful Natural Parks. For this new Cicerone edition of the guide I rewalked the 420 kilometres of the route for the fifth time. In some places the clearing of old paths meant the original walk could be improved and on another day a disputed access necessitated creating a new route. GR7 waymarking was already in place 10 years ago which has now been joined by GR249, GR245 and GR141 waymarking on several days. And it was gratifying to see that the increase in the number of walkers coming to Andalucía has been reflected in the opening of several new places to stay along the way: you'll find them listed in each of the village descriptions.

Each leg of this magnificent 21-day trail offers its own rich rewards. Moorish castles and Roman footpaths, hidden coves and ancient oak forests, friendly locals and great folk cuisine and the rugged beauty of Andalucía's Baetic mountains are but a few of the jewels that await you on this coast to coast odyssey.

Guy Hunter-Watts

El Burgo seen from the west (Day 11)

INTRODUCTION

The Sierra de Almijara seen from above Cómpeta (Day 1)

The Andalucían Coast to Coast Walk was inspired by a wish to create a long-distance walk linking the two great seas which cradle Andalucía. The route extends from Maro on the Mediterranean coast to Bolonia on the Atlantic, traversing the region's mountainous interior and connecting seven of Andalucía's most beautiful protected areas.

The Baetic system of mountains runs east to west across Andalucía like a mighty sabre, separated from the Sierra Morena to the north by the broad valley of the Guadalquivir. As it crosses the provinces of Granada and Jaen the massif splits into two branches: the Subbetic range to the north and the Penibetic range to the south. The latter chain is home to mainland Spain's highest peaks, with the Mulhacén rising 3457m above sea level.

The Coast to Coast Walk follows the Penibetic system as it runs across the provinces of Málaga, Granada and Cádiz before arcing south towards the Strait of Gibraltar, sticking mostly to its southern flank. Sections of the walk coincide with the GR7, others link in with parts of the GR249 or Gran Senda de Málaga while some legs share their route with sections of the GR141 and the GR245.

The 416km, 21-day trail leads you through stunning hilltop villages, past fascinating archaeological sites, along Berber footpaths, across Roman bridges, through deep gorges and over high passes. Should you walk the route in its entirety you'll have journeyed from sea to ocean through the heart of one of the most beautiful tracts of mountains in Europe.

If the Mediterranean gave Spain so much of its identity, it would be the Atlantic which would offer it a leading role on the world's stage. It was this temporal progression that made me decide to walk from east to west rather than vice versa. It also meant that for most of each walking day the sun would be behind you, rather than in your face. I wanted the route to link as many of southern Spain's Natural Parks as possible and for each leg to connect two villages, and that each day might be comfortably walked by anyone in good health. This meant that walkers following the trail would have the possibility to overnight in village accommodation rather than needing to carry camping gear.

This is a village to village walk, with an average daily distance of 20km and the longest day clocking in at a little over 26km. This means that each stage of the walk can comfortably be covered in a day with time to spare for exploring the beautiful villages through which the walk passes. There are few campsites along the way so most walkers who tackle the route choose to stay in hotels and pensions in the destination villages where there are plenty of options for all budgets. Few people will have the luxury of tackling all 21 days at one go, but the route can be walked over time as a series of day walks or divided into a number of shorter sections.

OTHER LONG-DISTANCE ROUTES THROUGH ANDALUCÍA

The **GR7/E4** footpath begins in Tarifa and ends in Athens, traversing the whole of Andalucía in its early stages. About a third of the way across southern Spain, the footpath divides into a northern and a southern variant, the latter looping all the way round the southern flank of the Sierra Nevada. The total length of all the Andalucían stages of the route is around 1200km.

The **GR249** or 'La Gran Senda de Málaga' is a more recent creation. The route describes a huge loop via the mountainous interior and the Mediterranean coast of one of Spain's most beautiful provinces. The route covers about half the distance of the Andalucían GR7, some 650km in total.

The early stages of the walk: La Costa Tropical and La Maroma massif

The walk's start point is the beach below the pretty village of Maro, about an hour's drive east of Málaga. You're at the heart of the Costa Tropical at a point where the Penibetic mountains rise steeply upwards, just a few kilometres in from the sea. Within an hour of leaving the coastal Paraje Natural you enter a second Natural Park where for the next four days you follow magnificent mountain paths and tracks westwards through the Sierra de Tejeda, Almijara y Alhama via some of the prettiest inland villages in Andalucía. The trail crosses the fertile terraces close to Frigiliana and Cómpeta where you pass through vineyards and groves of avocado, loquats and citrus that flourish in the region's sub-tropical climate.

The path loops up to a higher level as you follow a high trail round the rugged flank of La Maroma (2069m). When you consider that La Maroma's summit is almost 2500 feet higher than Ben Nevis you get an idea of just how grandiose the scenery that you'll encounter will be while the region's mild climate ensures that you'll rarely be battling against the forces of Nature.

Through the mountains north of Málaga: El Torcal and El Chorro

Leaving La Maroma's western reaches, after looping briefly north into Granada province, the scenery becomes less abrupt as the trail reverts to its westerly

Valle de Abdalajís seen in summer from the east (Day 9)

course. Running along the south side of the Sierra de Camarolos then on past the jagged karst limestone landscapes of the Torcal Park, the sub-tropical vegetation of the early stages of the walk gives way to olive groves and fields of wheat and barley. Here the trail dips in and out of the river valleys which cut through the sierras as they run south towards Málaga and the sea. This is where you pass by the towering cliff faces of El Chorro where the recently inaugurated Caminito del Rey – a dizzy walkway suspended high above the gorge – has become a major tourist attraction. You could split the tenth day of walking into two legs in order to hike this extraordinary path.

West through La Sierra de las Nieves to Ronda

Heading on west towards Ronda you next traverse the northern reaches of the Parque Natural de la Sierra de las Nieves. This is a wild, relatively unknown range of mountains that is soon to become a Parque Nacional with the additional kudos that the designation implies. Here, once again, you find yourself walking through a range of towering peaks that rise to almost 2000m. As the park's name implies you could see snow in winter even though it's exceptionally rare that this is heavy enough to thwart any walking plans.

After a long, steady climb up from El Burgo to the remote Puerto de Lifa you descend to reach a flatter stretch of track as you cross the vast, cultivated plain that lies east of Ronda.

Ronda is a destination in its own right and has long been a magnet for travellers from all corners of the globe. The town deserves its 'Town of Dreams' epithet with a physical location of rare beauty where palaces, convents and mansion houses cling to the precipitous sides of its famous gorge: its Puente Nuevo is among the most photographed monuments in Europe. Coming a little more than halfway through the walk Ronda might be a place to book a second night, taking a break from walking to explore the town's fascinating Moorish citadel.

South from Ronda into the Sierra de Grazalema

You leave Ronda by way of a spectacular path that zigzags down one side of its plunging gorge before it crosses a low pass to reach the Guadalevín valley and the Parque Natural de Grazalema.

Recently declared a UNESCO biosphere reserve the Grazalema park is home to no less than a third of the wildflowers in Spain and is one of the country's prime birding locations. As you head along the wild and little-known Líbar valley you're bound to be treated to the sight of dozens of griffon vultures (*Gyps fulvus*) riding the thermals that rise up the abrupt cliff faces on which they nest. The trail passes through another swathe of deeply weathered karst and past ancient stands of gall oak (*Quercus faginea*) and cork oak (*Quercus suber*) forest before you cross back to the Guadalevín valley to reach Cortes de la Frontera.

Through the heart of the Parque Natural de los Alcornocales to the sea
From Cortes down to the sea the trail coincides with sections of the GR7 and the GR141 as you head south through one of Europe's largest cork oak forests towards the sea. Highlights of this part of the walk include the deep gorge of Las Buitreras, the hilltop town of Jimena de la Frontera and the eerily beautiful, hilltop citadel of Castillo de Castellar.

The vegetation once again changes as you lose elevation and the influence of the Mediterranean becomes more marked. Groves of citrus, avocado and loquats reappear while ferns and mosses take the place of gorse and rosemary in the forest's *sotobosque* (the lower growth in a forest, ie that which lies beneath the canopy layer). At the park's southernmost edge the walk leads past a number of *canutos* (streambeds which have unusually diverse plant life, born of their moist, cloud forest-like climate.), home to a uniquely diverse ecosystem. Long views now open out south towards the Strait and, on clear days, to the mountains of North Africa.

Along the coast to Tarifa and the Atlantic, then on to Bolonia
After almost 400km of mountain trail the walk reaches the Mediterranean once again a few kilometres northwest of El Pelayo. Here you pick up the coastal drovers' path which you follow

The coastal path close to Tarifa (Day 20)

past a line of coastal fortifications to reach Tarifa and the Atlantic Ocean.

Tarifa has become one of Andalucía's most vibrant small towns since the arrival of a kite and wind-surfing community from all around the world and the town has several great restaurants and masses of places to stay.

The walk's final day is among its most memorable. From Tarifa you follow the ocean's edge, crossing the beaches of Los Lances and Valdevaqueros, to reach the tiny, oceanside settlement of Bolonia whose Roman ruins are among the best preserved in Spain. The village has a handful of mid-budget places to stay and some great fish restaurants.

PLANTS AND WILDLIFE

Two major highlights of any walk in southern Spain come in the form of the flowers and birds you see along the way.

HIGHLIGHTS OF THE COAST TO COAST WALK

Natural Parks
(described on an east to west basis)
• Paraje Natural de los Acantilados de Maro/Cerro Gordo
• Parque Natural de mijara y Alhama
• Parque Natural Sierra de las Nieves
• Parque Natural de la Sierra de Grazalema
• Parque Natural de los Alcornocales
• Parque Natural del Estrecho

Historical sites
• Bobastro: mountain refuge of renegade chieftain Omar Ibn Hafsun
• Carratraca: ancient spa settlement
• Ronda: the Puente Nuevo and Moorish citadel
• Castillo de Castellar: hilltop Moorish fort and Roman footpath
• La Casa de Piedra: early Christian church hewn from rock
• Tarifa: ancient walled town at the confluence of two seas
• Baelo Claudio: some of the best preserved Roman remains in Spain

Villages
Some of Andalucía's most beautiful villages including Maro, Frigiliana, Canillas de Albaída, Carratraca, Ronda, Montejaque, Castillo de Castellar and Jimena de la Frontera.

Andalucía numbers among the finest birding destinations in Europe and ornithological tourism has grown rapidly in recent years. The best time for birdwatching is during the spring and autumn migrations between Europe and North Africa – you walk directly beneath the main migratory route at the end of the Coast to Coast Walk – but at any time of year you can expect rich birdlife.

Several species of eagle are commonly seen and you're guaranteed sightings of soaring griffon vultures – sometimes a hundred or more – which nest in the deep gorges at El Chorro and El Colmenar. As well as seasonal visitors there are more than 250 species present throughout the year.

If you'd like a list of the more common species visit www.cicerone.co.uk/970/resources.

Pink Butterfly Orchid, *Orchis papilionacea*

For further information about birding resources and organised birding tours and walks, see Appendix A (Useful contacts).

Ibex, *Capra pyrenaica hispanica*

The mountains and valleys through which the walk passes also offer rich rewards for botanists. Some 40% of all species found in Iberia are present in Andalucía and many of these are to be found within these mountains including a number of endemic species. The annual wild-flower explosion in late spring is as spectacular as anywhere in southern Europe, especially in areas where the rural exodus has ensured that much of the land has never seen the use of pesticides.

For a list of 300 of the more common species to be found in Andalucía, with common and Latin names, visit www.cicerone.co.uk/970/resources.

Vertebrates are less easy to spot but are also present. Along with the grazing goats, sheep, cattle and Iberian pigs, you may see squirrels, hares, rabbits, stoat, deer, wild boar, otters and mongoose. Ibex (*Capra pyrenaica hispanica*) are making a rapid comeback in Andalucía and these can often be spotted on the southern flanks of La Maroma which you traverse early in the walk. The dense oak forests of Los Alcornocales are home to large numbers of deer, and you'll have a good chance of observing them between Jimena de la Frontera and El Colmenar as well as in the forests and canutos south of Los Barrios.

Appendix C (Further reading) includes details of guidebooks that will help you to identify the plants and wildlife of the region.

ANDALUCÍA: THE HISTORICAL CONTEXT

Anyone who has travelled to other parts of the Iberian Peninsula will be aware of the marked differences between the regions of Spain and its peoples. If Franco sought to impose a centralist and authoritarian system of government on his people in the New Spain, ushered in with the departure of El Caudillo and the advent of liberal democracy, most Spaniards actively celebrate the country's diverse, multi-lingual and multi-faceted culture.

But if Spain is different, as the marketing campaigns of the 90s and noughties would have us believe, then Andalucía is even more so. It is,

Statue of the Emperor Trajan, Baelo Claudio (Day 21)

of course, about much more than the stereotypical images of flamenco, fiestas, castanets, flounced dresses, sherry and bullfighting: any attempt to define what constitutes the Andaluz character must probe far deeper. But what very quickly becomes apparent on any visit to the region is that this is a place of ebullience, joie de vivre, easy conversation and generous gestures. Andalucíans tend to be gregarious and generous, and invariably offer a genuinely warm welcomes to visitors from abroad.

What goes to make such openness of character is inextricably linked to the region's history and its geographical position at the extreme south of Europe, looking east to the rest of Europe, west to the Atlantic and with just a short stretch of water separating its southernmost tip from Africa. This is a land at the crossroads between two continents, at the same time part of one of the richest spheres of trade the world has ever known: the Mediterranean Basin. Visitors from faraway places are nothing new.

A thousand years before Christ, the minerals and rich agricultural lands of Andalucía had already attracted the interest of the Phoenicians, who established trading posts in Málaga and Cádiz. But it was under the Romans, who ruled Spain from the 3rd century BC to the 5th century AD that the region began to take on its present-day character. They established copper and silver mines, planted olives and vines, cleared land for agriculture and built towns, roads, aqueducts, bridges, theatres and baths while imposing their native language and customs. Incursions by Vandals and then Visigoths ended their rule, but their legacy was to be both rich and enduring.

The arrival of the Moors
If Rome laid the foundations of Andalucían society in its broadest sense, they were shallow in comparison to those that would be bequeathed in the wake of the expeditionary force that sailed across the Strait in 711 under the Moorish commander Tariq.

After the death of the Prophet, Islam had spread rapidly through the Middle East and across the north of Africa, and the time was ripe for taking it into Europe. Landing close to Gibraltar, Tariq's army decisively defeated the ruling Visigoths in their first encounter. What had been little more than a loose confederation of tribes, deprived of their ruler, offered little resistance to the advance of Islam across Spain. It was only when Charles Martel defeated the Moorish army close to the banks of the Loire in 732 that the tide began to turn and the Moors looked to consolidate their conquests rather than venture deeper into Europe.

A first great capital was established at Toledo, and it became clear that the Moors had no plans to leave in a hurry: Andalucía was to become part of an Islamic state for almost eight centuries. Moorish Spain's golden age took hold in the 8th century, when Jews, Christians and Moors established a modus vivendi the likes of which has rarely been replicated, and which yielded one of the richest artistic periods Europe has known. Philosophers, musicians, poets, mathematicians and astronomers from all three religions helped establish Córdoba as a centre for learning second to no other in the West, at the centre of a trading network that stretched from Africa to the Middle East and through Spain to northern Europe.

However, the Moorish Kingdom was always under threat, and the Reconquest – a process that was to last more than 800 years – gradually gained momentum as the Christian kingdoms of central and northern Spain became more unified. Córdoba

fell in 1031, Seville in 1248, and the great Caliphate splintered into a number of smaller Taifa kingdoms. The Moors clung on for another 250 years: the settlements along 'la frontera' fell in the early 1480s, and finally, after the fall of Granada in 1492, the whole of Spain was once again under Christian rule.

Spain's Golden Age

If ever anybody was in the right place at the right time, it was the Genoese adventurer Cristóbal Colon, aka Christopher Columbus, who was in the Christian camp at Santa Fe when Granada capitulated. His petition to the Catholic monarchs for funding for an expedition to sail west in order to reach the East fell on fertile soil.

The discovery of America, and along with it the fabulous riches that would make their way back to a Spain newly united under Habsburg rule, was to usher in Spain's *Siglo de Oro* or Golden Age. Spain's empire would soon stretch from the Caribbean through Central and South America and on to the Philippines; riches flowed back from the colonies at a time when Seville and Cádiz numbered among the wealthiest cities in Europe. The most obvious manifestation of this wealth – and nowhere more so than in Andalucía – were the palaces, churches, monasteries and convents that were built during this period: never again would the country see such generous patronage of the Arts.

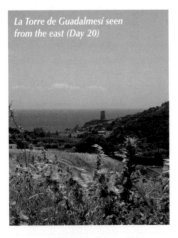

La Torre de Guadalmesí seen from the east (Day 20)

However, by the end of the 16th century Spain's position at the centre of the world stage was under threat. A series of wars in Europe depleted Spain's credibility as well as the state coffers: by the late 17th century Spanish power was in free fall. It remained a spent force into the 19th century, and yet further violent conflict in the early 20th century led to General Francisco Franco ('El Caudillo') sweeping into power in 1936.

The modern era

Franco embarked on a 'crusade' to re-establish the traditional order in Spain. The ensuing conflict – the Spanish Civil War – lasted for three years, during which an estimated 500,000 Spaniards lost their lives. The eventual victory of the Nationalists in 1939 led to Franco's consolidation and centralisation of power and the establishment of an authoritarian state that remained until his death in 1975.

Franco had hoped that King Juan Carlos, who he'd appointed as his successor prior to his death, would continue to govern much in his image; but the young king knew which way the tide was running and immediately began to facilitate the creation of a new constitution for Spain and, along with it, parliamentary democracy. Andalucía, as was the case for several other regions of Spain, saw the creation of an autonomous Junta, or government, based in Seville.

The 80s, 90s and noughties were very good years for Andalucía, following Spain's entry into the EEC,

Descending towards the Roman bridge at Sedella (Day 3)

Spanish Festoon butterfly
(Zerynthia rumina)

and these decades saw its infra-structure rapidly transformed. New roads, schools, hospitals and hotels were built, along with a high-speed train line from Seville to Madrid. The huge construction boom put money into many a working person's pocket; Andalucía had never had it so good.

Tourism continues to be a major motor of the Andalucían economy, along with the construction industry, fuelled by expats setting up home in the south and other foreigners buying holiday homes and flats. But the economic downturn hit the region hard and Andalucía currently has an unemployment rate among its adult workforce of almost 35% while among young people that percentage is almost double.

At the time of writing there are signs that the building industry – a yardstick for the rest of the economy – is beginning to recover and that a naturally optimistic people are beginning to believe that the worst is behind them. The numbers of foreign visitors to the country continues to grow while most Spaniards remain committed to forging a multicultural and unified Europe

GETTING THERE

By air
Málaga is the closest airport to the walk's start point and has charter flights from all major cities in the UK as well as scheduled flights with British Airlines and Iberia.

For the middle to end section of the walk Jerez or Seville would be closer than Málaga while for the final five days Gibraltar would be the nearest airport.

By car
Car hire in Spain is inexpensive when compared to that in other European destinations, and the major compa-nies are represented at all airports. Prices for car hire from Málaga tend to be lower. You could drive to any of the Walk stages' start points and return later in the day by taxi or, in a couple of cases, by train.

By train and bus
All of the villages along the Coast to Coast Walk can be accessed by bus. See listings in Appendix A.

You could take a train (then in some cases a short taxi ride) to pick up the start points of Days 13 to 19.

Getting to Maro
The easiest way to get to Maro from Málaga, the nearest major airport to the Coast to Coast's start point, is by bus from the city's main bus station. A shuttle bus between the airport and the bus station departs every

20–25 minutes between 7am and midnight.

Buses depart for Nerja, 3km west of Maro, every hour between 7am and 10pm. The journey takes between 60 and 90 minutes depending on the number of stops.

There are few buses from Nerja to Maro. A short 10-minute transfer by taxi costs between €10 and €15.

Getting from Bolonia
From Bolonia, the end point of the Coast to Coast Walk, there is only a very limited bus service so you're best to leave by taxi to Algeciras or Tarifa then travel onwards by bus. There are regular departures throughout the day for both Seville and Málaga as well as a less regular service to Jerez.

LUGGAGE TRANSFERS BY TAXI

One option for walking the route is to take normal luggage and then have your bag(s) moved on by taxi, allowing you the luxury of walking with just a day pack. I've listed taxi contact numbers for all villages, and hotel owners can often help out.

In 2018 the cost of this service would average around €30 per transfer. When shared two ways it wouldn't add too much to the overall cost of your hike.

The track leading towards El Puente de los Alemanes after heavy rain (Day 15)

WHEN TO GO

As a general rule, the best time to walk in Andalucía is from March through to June and from September to late October. This is when you're likely to encounter mild, sunny weather: warm enough to dine al fresco yet not so hot as to make temperature an additional challenge. Wildflowers are at their best in late April/early May and this is the time when many walking companies plan their walks.

Most walkers avoid July and August when temperatures regularly reach the mid to high 30s, making walking much more of a challenge.

If you're prepared to risk seeing some rain then winter is a wonderful time to be out walking in Andalucía, especially from December to February when rainfall is generally less than in November, March and April.

ACCOMMODATION

If Andalucían tourism was once all about beach and hotel tourism the past 30 years have seen a huge growth in the numbers of visitors who come to discover its walking trails. Prices in the mountains are generally low in comparison to the hotels of the coastal resorts. As a rule of thumb, for €50–€75 you'll find a decent hotel room for two with its own bath or shower room and breakfast will often be included.

Contact details of recommended hotels, hostels and B&Bs are provided for all the stage finish points. Most offer breakfast and some evening meals while many places can prepare picnics given prior warning.

Nearly every hotel in Andalucía is listed on www.booking.com, where, in theory, you'll always get the lowest

Following the northern slopes of the Sierra de Prieta towards El Burgo (Day 11)

price. Bear in mind that by contacting the hotel directly you'll be saving them the commission they'd pay to the website: they're sometimes happy to cut out the third party and offer a lower price. However, both booking.com and TripAdvisor (www.tripadvisor.co.uk) can be good starting points for planning your walk. If the hotels recommended in some of the more remote villages are fully booked you might consider staying in an apartment. In this case Airbnb (www.airbnb.es) is a good starting point.

When sleeping in budget options during cold weather it's worth ringing ahead to ask the owners if they'd mind switching on the heating before your arrival. Remember, too, that cheaper hostels often don't provide soap or shampoo.

When checking in expect to be asked for your passport. Once details have been noted down, Spanish law requires that it's returned to you.

Camping
There are very few campsites along the route. Wild camping is generally tolerated in Andalucía and you could find places to pitch a tent close to the end point of all stages.

EATING OUT IN SOUTHERN SPAIN
Although it may not be known as a gourmet destination, you can eat well in Andalucía if you're prepared to leave a few preconceptions at home. Much of the food on menus in mountain village restaurants is stored in a deep freezer and microwaved when ordered, while *tapas* are freshly prepared and displayed in a glass cabinet in most bars and restaurants. These can provide a delicious meal in themselves.

A tapa (taking its name from the lid or 'tapa' that once covered the jars in which they were stored) has come to mean a saucer-sized plate of any one dish, served to accompany an aperitif before lunch or dinner. If you wish to have more of any particular tapa you can order a *ración* (a large plateful) or a *media ración* (half that amount). Two or three raciónes shared between two, along with the ubiquitous mixed salad, would make a substantial and inexpensive meal.

When eating à la carte don't expect there to be much in the way of vegetables served with any meal: they just don't tend to figure in Andalusian cuisine. However, no meal in southern Spain is complete without some form of salad, and fresh fruit is always available as a dessert.

Bear in mind that there's always a *menú del día* (set menu) available at lunchtime and as a result of the economic downturn some restaurants now offer the menú del día in the evenings. Although you have less choice – generally two or three starters, mains and desserts – set menus are often prepared on the day, using fresh rather than frozen ingredients.

Expect to pay around €10 for a set menu in a village restaurant which

29

normally includes a soft drink, beer or a glass of wine. When eating à la carte you can expect to pay more like €20–€25 per head for a three-course meal including beverages, while a tapas style meal would be rather less. Tipping is common although no offence will be taken should you not leave a gratuity.

The southern Spanish eat later than is the custom in northern Europe. Lunch isn't generally available until 2.00pm and restaurants rarely open before 7.00pm. A common lament among walkers is that breakfast is often not served at hotels until 9.00am, although village bars are open from 8am. If you're keen to make an early start you could always buy the makings of your own breakfast from a village shop the day before.

Breakfasts in hotels can be disappointing and is often better taken at a local bar. Most serve better coffee than you'll get at a hotel, freshly squeezed rather than boxed orange juice, and *una tostada con aceite y tomate* – toast served with tomato and olive oil – can be a great way to start your walking day.

Be aware that village shops are generally open from 9.00am to 2.00pm and then 5.30pm to 8.30pm. Many smaller shops will make you up a *bocadillo* or sandwich using the ingredients of your choice.

LANGUAGE

Visitors to inland Andalucía often express surprise at how little English is spoken, where even in restaurants and hotels a working knowledge of English is the exception rather than the norm. In addition, the Spanish spoken in southern Spain – Andaluz

The fertile plain between La Sierra de las Nieves and Ronda (Day 12)

– can be difficult to understand even if you have a command of basic Spanish: it's spoken at lightning speed, with the end of words often left unpronounced.

It's worth picking up a phrasebook before you travel. And be prepared to gesticulate: you always get there in the end.

MONEY

Most travellers to Spain still consider that the cost of their holiday essentials – food, travel and accommodation – is considerably lower than in northern Europe. You can still find a decent meal for two, with drinks, for around €40; and €60 can buy you a comfortable hotel room for two.

Every village along the Coast to Coast Walk has an ATM apart from El Pelayo and Bolonia and you'll generally be able to pay with a credit card in shops, restaurants and hotels. Be aware that you'll often be asked for credit card details when booking a hotel room by phone.

COMMUNICATIONS

While most of Spain now has good mobile coverage for all major phone operators, there are still quite a few gaps in the mountains where many of these stages will be taking you. Even so, it's always wise to have a charged phone in your pack, preloaded with emergency contact numbers (see Appendix A, Useful contacts).

Wifi coverage is available in nearly all hotels in Andalucía.

WHAT TO TAKE

The two most important things to take with you when you walk in Andalucía are:

- water - carry a minimum of two litres. During the warmer months the greatest potential dangers are heat exhaustion and dehydration. Wear loose-fitting clothes, a hat, and keep drinking.
- comfortable, broken-in walking boots – no walk is enjoyable when you've got blisters.

With safety in mind, you should also carry the following:

- hat and sun block
- map and compass
- Swiss Army Knife or similar
- torch and whistle
- fully charged mobile phone (even though coverage can be patchy in the mountains)
- waterproofs, according to season
- fleece or jumper (temperatures can drop rapidly at the top of the higher passes)
- first aid kit including antihistamine cream, plasters, bandage, plastic skin for blisters
- water purifying tablets
- chocolate/sweets or glucose tablets
- handheld GPS device (if you have one)

31

GR waymarking en route to Ronda (Day 12)

MAPS

In the summary of each stage I've recommended the IGN map(s) which cover(s) that particular leg, and Appendix A includes the contact details of companies (both in the UK and in Spain) from which you can buy these maps. All of the Spanish retailers will send maps *contra reembolso* (payment on receipt) to addresses within Spain.

STAYING SAFE

Log the following emergency telephone numbers into your mobile:

- 112 Emergency services general number
- 062 Guardía Civil (police)
- 061 Medical emergencies
- 080 Fire brigade

In addition to the usual precautions you would take, there are a few things to remember when walking in Andalucía:

- **Water** – Springs which normally have water throughout the year are mentioned in the text. But do note that in dry years, like the one when this guidebook was written and researched, these springs could have slowed to a trickle or be totally dry. Always carry plenty of water, and consider keeping a supply of water purification tablets in your daypack.
- **Fire** – in the dry months the hillsides of Andalucía become a vast tinderbox. Be very careful if you smoke or use a camping stove.
- **Hunting areas** – signs for '*coto*' or '*coto privado de caza*' designate

an area where hunting is permitted in season and not that you're entering private property. Cotos are normally marked by a small rectangular sign divided into a white-and-black triangle.

- **Close all gates** – you'll come across some extraordinary gate-closing devices! They can take time, patience and effort to open and close.

USING THIS GUIDE

The information boxes at the start of each stage of the walk provide the essential statistics: start point, total distance covered, ascent and descent, grade or rating and estimated walking time. They also include en route refreshments options. The subsequent stage introduction gives you a feel for what any given itinerary involves.

The € symbols next to each hotel/ accommodation listing give you a rough idea of what you might expect to pay.

€ less than €50 for 2
€€ between €50 and €100 for 2
€€€ more than €100 for 2

The route description, together with the individual route map, should allow you to follow each stage of the walk without difficulty. However, do note that not all stage maps use the same scale. Places and features on the map are highlighted in bold in the route description to aid navigation. However, you should always carry a compass and, ideally, the

recommended map of the area; and a handheld GPS device is always an excellent second point of reference (see 'GPS tracks', below).

Water springs have been included in the route descriptions but bear in mind that following dry periods (at the time of writing this guide in 2017 Andalucía is experiencing one of the driest years on record) they may be all but non-existent.

Grading

The stages are graded as follows:

- Easy/Medium – mid-length walks with little steep climbing
- Medium – mid-length walks with some steep uphill and downhill sections
- Medium/Difficult – longer routes with some steep uphill and downhill sections
- Difficult – long routes with long and challenging uphill and downhill sections

If you're reasonably fit you should experience no difficulty with any of these routes. For stages classed as Medium/Difficult, the most important thing is to allow plenty of time and take a good supply of water. For the stages classed as Difficult, you should aim to set out earlier in the day and preferably straight after breakfast. And remember that what can be an easy walk in cooler weather becomes a much more difficult challenge in the heat. This rating system assumes the sort of weather you're likely to encounter in winter, spring or autumn in Andalucía.

Looking west in the evening light from Alcaucín (Day 4)

Time

These timings are based on an average walking pace, without breaks. You'll soon see if it equates roughly to your own pace, and can then adjust timings accordingly. On all routes allow an additional hour-and-a-half or so if you intend to break for food, photography and rest stops.

Definition of terms

The terms used in this guide are intended to be as unambiguous as possible. In route descriptions, 'track' denotes any thoroughfare wide enough to permit vehicle access, and 'path' is used to describe any that is wide enough only for pedestrians and animals.

You'll see references in many stages to 'GR' and 'PR'. GR stands for Gran Recorrido or long-distance footpath; these routes are marked with red and white waymarking. PR stands for Pequeño Recorrido or short-distance footpath and these routes are marked with yellow-and-white waymarking.

A glossary of Spanish terms used in the route description can be found in Appendix B.

GPS tracks

The GPX trail files for all 21 days of the Coast to Coast Walk are available as free downloads from Cicerone (www.cicerone.co.uk/970/GPX) and via the author's website (www.guy-hunterwatts.com – simply request the files via the 'Contact' page).

By using a programme such as Garmin's BaseCamp you can download the files to your desktop, import them into the programme and then transfer them to your handheld device. You can download Basecamp for Mac and PC at www.garmin.com/garmin/cms/us/onthetrail/basecamp.

GPX files are provided in good faith, but neither the author nor Cicerone can accept responsibility for their accuracy. Your first point of reference should always be the walking notes themselves.

THE ROUTE

The southern flank of La Maroma (Day 4)

DAY 1
Maro to Frigiliana

Start	Maro beach – follow the N-340 east along the top of the village to a roundabout then follow signs for 'Playa' down past El Ingenio to the beach
Distance	15.2km
Ascent/Descent	930m/660m
Grade	Medium/Difficult
Time	5hr 35min
Map	ING 1:50000 Motril 1055 & Vélez-Málaga 1054
Refreshments	Bar at entrance to Cueva de Nerja early in the walk

The Coast to Coast Walk's start point is the beach which lies just beneath Maro, one of the prettiest villages of the Costa Tropical, next to the Mediterranean Sea.

After climbing up to the village the day begins in gentle mode as you follow a broad forestry track that runs north from the Cueva de Nerja towards the Sierra de Almijara.

Passing the picnic area at El Pinarillo things take on a different tempo as the trail roller coasters its way west across four deep gorges towards Frigiliana. It hardly seems possible, walking through such wild mountain scenery, that you're only a few kilometres from the urban sprawl of the coastal resorts.

The Nerja Cave is worth a detour if you've set out early in the day (see Maro section, below).

MARO (POPULATION 741, ALTITUDE 122M)

Maro numbers among the most attractive villages along Andalucía's Mediterranean seaboard. The town lies at the eastern end of the area that the Moors knew as La Axarquía, meaning Land to the East, as opposed to Algarve meaning Land to the West. Just three kilometres east of the busy resort of Nerja the village has a much sleepier feel than its neighbour and has escaped the development which has blighted so much of the Costa del Sol. Even in summer you can still stake a claim on the beaches close to the village while for the remainder of the year they are pretty much deserted.

The village had its moment of glory when the surrounding land was planted with cane for sugar manufacture: the region's mild, sub-tropical climate was perfect for growing the crop (you pass the old *ingenio*, where sugar was made, early on Day 1 of the the Coast to Coast Walk). This flourishing industry, which began in the 16th century, rapidly declined in the last century when it proved unable to compete in price with sugar manufactured from beet.

The arrival of an expat community from the 1960s onwards helped revive the place's fortunes while much of the land surrounding the village remained in the hands of the Larios family. Their reluctance to develop their estates kept the developers at bay until the stretch of coast lying to either side of the village was declared a protected area.

The Nerja Cave, a complex of underground caverns and lakes that was discovered in 1959 by a group of schoolboys hunting for bats, lies just behind the village. Music and dance events are held here every year and have attracted world-renowned artists such as Montserrat Caballé and Paco de Lucía. The caves are worth a visit: you pass the entrance gate half an hour into the first day of walking.

From a balconied walkway, La Maravilla, which arcs round the southern side of the village, there are fine views across open fields to the Mediterranean. Take a stroll here at sunset, at the time of the evening *paseo* (village stroll), to get a feel for Maro's heady charms.

Recommended accommodation

Hotel Restaurante Playa Maro €–€€
www.hotelplayamaro.com
On the eastern side of the village with swimming pool.

Hotel Al-Andalus €€
www.lorenzoreche.net
Close to La Cueva de Maro though within earshot of the motorway.

Apartamentos Balcón de Maro €€
Simple studio apartments, some with sea views. All reservations taken via **www.booking.com**

Contacts

Nerja Cave: **www.cuevadenerja.es** (summer 10am–7.30pm, winter 10am–2pm, 4pm–6.30pm)
Tourist Office: **www.nerja.es**
Taxi: rank in Nerja at 3km, 952 520 537

The beach at Maro, start point of the Coast to Coast Walk

You have 416km (258 miles) of trail ahead of you.

The walk begins on the Playa de Maro next to the life-guard's chair. ◄

Head west past the beach's shower then cut right up a flight of steps. At the top bear left to reach a parking area then follow a narrow road up past a number

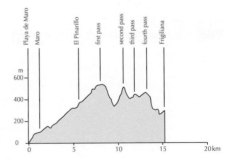

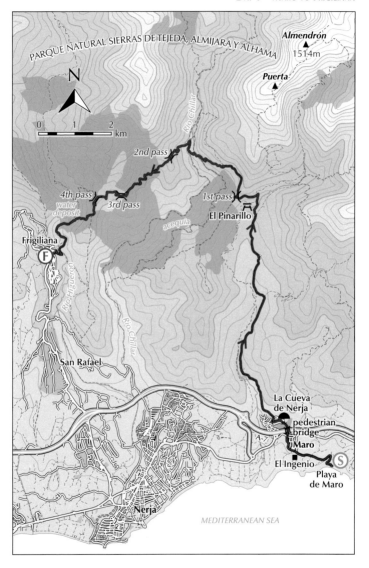

of greenhouses to the village. The road levels as it runs towards the ruined structure of El Ingenio (see Maro section).

Here turn left up a flight of steps which leads past **El Ingenio** to reach a road and La Plaza Iglesia de Maro. Continue straight ahead along Calle Virgen de las Maravillas. The road arcs round Maro's southern flank with a balustraded walkway running to its left. Looping right then once more left past a 'No Entry' sign, then bearing once more right, you reach a junction opposite Bar La Entrada. Head directly across the road, still along Calle Virgen de las Maravillas. Where the street cuts right continue straight ahead then cross a **pedestrian bridge** over the A-7 motorway. Beyond the bridge a looping path leads up through a botanical garden to the car park of **La Cueva de Nerja** (**25min**). Bear left, exit the car park gates then turn immediately right following a sign 'Área Recreativa El Pinarillo' and GR249 waymarking.

After 75m you pass a green barrier. Head straight on along a broad forestry track which climbs gradually upwards, marked by GR249 posts. Reaching a fork where one sign points left for 'Área Recreativa El Pinarillo' and another right for 'Sendero' branch left. The track continues to climb before arriving at **El Pinarillo** (**1hr 45min**) where it divides once again. Here angle left past a map of the park then head straight through the **picnic area** past a row of barbecues following GR249 waymarking. Passing a threshing circle continue past a green barrier then drop down a broad track and cross a riverbed.

20m beyond the riverbed the track divides. Take the narrower, left-hand path which climbs steeply and shortly crosses the track you've just left. Heading on up a deeply eroded path you reach a broader track. Here turn left and follow the track up to the top of the **first pass** where it passes a 'No Entry' sign. ◄

Continue along the track which angles hard right as you pass a chain blocking vehicle access. After 950m, where the track bears right, turn left down a narrow path which zigzags steeply into the Chillar gorge. The path

Soaring views open out to the north and west.

descends past a small ruin, crosses a water channel, then loops down to the riverbed (**2hr 50min**).

At a marker post bear right along the river's east bank for 40m then cross to the opposite bank via stepping stones: look for GR paint flashes on a rock. Cutting right along the river's west bank for about 50m the path angles left and climbs steeply before dividing by a marker post. ▶ Take the left fork and continue to climb to reach the top of the **second pass** of the stage (**3hr 30min**).

Beyond the pass the path, eroded in parts, descends into the next valley, soon crossing a streambed. It then climbs for a short distance before descending again and crossing another stream where there's a cairn and a marker post. Crossing two more streambeds it climbs to the top of a **third pass** where views open out into the next valley. The vegetation becomes sparser, the result of a forest fire in the recent past.

The path again descends and crosses another streambed before climbing to the top of the fourth and final **pass** from where the valley of the Río Higuerón is visible

Looking northwest towards the Sierra de Almijara

There are rock pools to your right where you can take a dip in the warmer months.

41

to the west. Here it runs along the spine of the ridge. Passing a marker post where there are views both east and west, it runs gently downhill just east of the ridge to reach a divide by a marker post (**4hr 40min**).

Here turn right down a narrow path which loops down through a stand of pines to reach the valley floor and a sign for 'Frigiliana/Fuente del Esparto'. Bearing left and descending you pass a white hut then a fenced **water deposit**. The track leads on down the valley then loops across to the river's west bank where it becomes concreted. Following the track steeply upwards through groves of avocado you reach the edge of the village, then the Unicaja bank and, just beyond, the Plaza del Ingenio and the Frigiliana taxi rank (**5hr 35min**).

FRIGILIANA (POPULATION 3039, ALTITUDE 345M)

Frigilana seen from the south with El Fuerte to the left

Frigiliana numbers among Andalucía's prettiest villages and has won numerous prizes and accolades. Geranium-clad balconies and narrow streets climb organically from its diminutive main square while the stunning gorges and crystalline waters of the Sierra de Enmedio are within easy walking distance of the village.

The village's fortunes, like those of Maro, were linked to the processing of sugar cane. Frigiliana had its own *ingenio* (factory where molasses and sugar were made) while paper was also produced from the resulting pulp. Thanks to the region's sub-tropical climate the terraced hillsides surrounding the village have been cultivated since Roman times while the Moors built an elaborate series of *acequias* (water channels) to bring water down from the Sierra de Almijara. Stretching out from the village are groves of fig, almond, olive and avocado as well as extensive vineyards: like neighbouring Cómpeta the village is known for its sweet moscatel wine and its *uvas pasas* (sun-dried raisins).

In a more recent chapter of its history Frigiliana has attracted a flow of day trippers from the resorts of the Costa del Sol as well as an influx of foreign residents: expect to hear a fair amount of English being spoken in its bars and restaurants. The tightly clustered houses of the old village are evocative of its Moorish past and it's in keeping that it was recently twinned with Chefchaouen in the Moroccan Rif. This region was to see some of the last *Morisco* (relating to the Moors who remained in Spain after the Reconquest) uprisings. The Moslems who stayed on after the Reconquest knew they were living on borrowed time yet were loath to abandon this exquisite swathe of Al Andalus. Taking refuge atop the rocky pinnacle of El Fuerte, just west of the village, their last stand in 1569 against de Zuarzo's troops is one of the most evocative incidents of the rebellion.

The village has adopted the epithet *Pueblo de las Tres Culturas* in recognition of its Islamic, Jewish and Christian past: its annual Festival de las 3 Culturas is an inspiring celebration of cultural diversity.

Recommended accommodation

Hospedería El Caravansarv €€
www.hospederia-el-caravansar-frigiliana.es
A cosy B&B 5min from Plaza del Ingenio

Hotel Villa Frigiliana €€
www.hotelvillafrigiliana.com
Large hotel at the entrance of the village.

Las Chinas €
www.hotel-laschinas.com
Simple family-run hotel with home cooking on the south side of the village.

Contacts

Ayuntamiento: **www.frigiliana.es**
Tourist Office: **www.turismofrigiliana.es**
Taxi: Paulino 696 969 469

DAY 2

Frigiliana to Cómpeta

Start	La Plaza del Ingenio, Frigiliana
Distance	18.5km
Ascent/Descent	915m/615m
Grade	Medium/Difficult
Time	6hr
Map	IGN 1:50000 Vélez-Málaga 1054 & Zafarraya 1040
Refreshments	El Acebuchal at 2hr 20min

The second day of the Coast to Coast Walk links two of La Axarquía's prettiest villages and takes you through another stunning slice of the Sierra de Almijara. Leaving Frigiliana by way of its pretty Calle Real a steep but short climb takes you up to a track that runs westwards beneath the high massif of El Fuerte.

After passing through the hamlet of El Acebuchal the track loops over a ridge to reach the next valley. Here you descend to the Patamalara river and the Fábrica de Luz de Cómpeta where the village's electricity was once generated.

From the valley floor steel yourself for long climb to the stage's highest point, the Collado pass, though from here it's downhill all the way to Cómpeta.

Great views, varied vegetation and the chance of cooling off in the Patamalara in the warmer months all make for an exceptional walk.

Be sure to spend a couple of euros to see the hilarious puppet show.

The stage begins in the Plaza del Ingenio next to a round hut which houses a puppet theatre. ◄ With your back to the hut turn left and head up the cobbled street beneath El Ingenio passing four ceramic tiled plaques. Head straight along Frigiliana's pretty Calle Real. Keeping left at a first fork follow Calle Real on through the village passing La Iglesia de San Antonio then the police station. At the street's far end cobbling gives way to tarmac as you pass a supermarket then a group of modern buildings before reaching a junction.

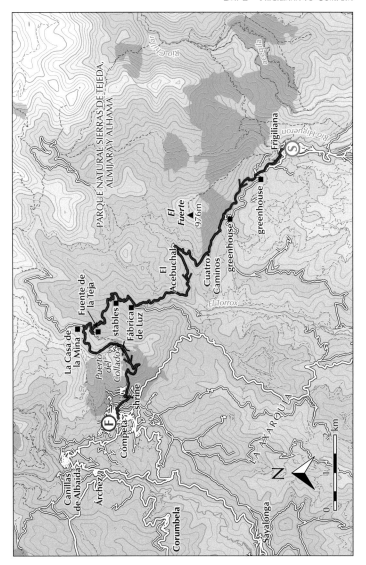

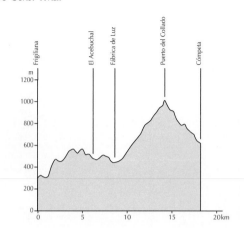

Turn right and follow a sign for Restaurante El Cortijo. Ignoring GR249 waymarking continue past Restaurante Santo Cristo then after 150m cut left up a steep footpath which climbs past a carob tree then meets the road once more. Turn left and after 30m cross the road and climb a bank just to the right of a black water pipe.

A narrow footpath zigzags steeply up through the rosemary and cistus: it's overgrown in parts but cairns and faded blue dots mark your way. The path loops left, passes above a **greenhouse** then angles back right and zigzags on up. Reaching the ridgetop the path bears left, levels, then runs up to a dirt track (**45min**). Here turn left.

After 35m you reach a fork. Keep left and head along a broad track which cuts through an abandoned olive grove then begins to gently descend. Passing a modern villa the track runs towards a grey metal gate and divides. Here bear right. The track becomes concreted in parts as it continues its descent, gradually contouring round the mountain.

At a point where the track angles hard left towards the road and another **greenhouse** go right into the bed of a narrow gorge. After 15m turn left up the bank and climb an indistinct footpath towards an ochre-coloured outcrop. Here angle left, parallel to a stand of pine trees which are to your left. The path, steep and loose, leads up to a sign for 'Parque Natural' then reaches a track where you should turn left. After 100m the track meets an asphalt road.

Maintain your course past a villa signed 'La Calera'. The road runs past the gates of several more houses as GR249 waymarking reappears. Passing by a sign marking a footpath leading to El Fuerte the road levels before it gently descends past a wall made of huge boulders then reaches a crossroads at **Cuatro Caminos**.

Bear right following a sign 'El Acebuchal', sticking to the main track which, running on through pines, reaches a fork. Here cut left following GR249 waymarking. Passing an isolated building the track descends to the valley floor where it arcs hard left before passing a shrine dedicated to San Judeos Tadeo. Passing between the two restaurants of **El Acebuchal** (**2hr 20min**) head on past the chapel of San Antonio.

El Acebuchal

You shortly pass by a huge carob tree then a second cluster of buildings. After a steady climb the track loops right, levels, then descends into the next valley. Eventually you reach the riverbed where another track runs to meet yours from the left (**3hr 5min**).

Head straight on along the riverbed. The track runs past the **Fábrica de Luz**, a former generating station. Cross the river via a footbridge then bear right and continue along the track which begins to ascend, looping past a high, breeze-block wall. Climbing steadily through olive groves you pass some **stables**, Los Olivillos.

Reaching a fork where one track leads down towards a line of eucalyptus, take the right, higher option. Passing a point where there are cypress trees to either side the track loops up to reach another fork, a few metres before **La Fuente de la Teja**. Again, take the right-hand option. The track arcs right before climbing steeply up to **La Casa de la Mina** where you reach a junction by a tennis court (**4hr 20min**).

La Fuente de la Teja

Turn left to follow a broad forestry track which runs up to the **Puerto del Collado**. After passing a forestry building with picnic benches you reach the top of the pass (890m). Ignoring a track which cuts up right, directly opposite the sign for 'Puerto del Collado', continue along main track which descends through a swathe of mountainside whose pine forest was rased to the ground by a forest fire in 2014. Looping right it passes an isolated villa before reaching the first houses above Cómpeta where you pass a ceramic sign 'Cruz del Monte'. The track soon arcs left, now concreted, before bearing back to the right then passing a mountain **shrine**. Descending past more villas the track reaches a junction.

Continue straight ahead following signs for 'Plaza de Vendimia' and 'Plaza del Carmen' and drop down a concrete track which, angling right, reaches another junction. Bear hard left and continue your descent to the Plaza de la Vendimia. Cross the square and continue down Calle Toledo then Calle Plazoleta. Reaching a tiny square with a fountain, turn right. The street bears left, right, then left again to reach a junction. Here cut left down Calle Carreterillas to reach the main square of **Cómpeta**, La Plaza de La Almijara (**6hr**).

CÓMPETA (POPULATION 3705, ALTITUDE 643M)

Cradled by the Sierra de Tejeda's southern slopes Cómpeta's labyrinth of narrow streets fans out from its pretty main square, La Plaza de Almijara. The village's principal landmark is the high, *neo-mudéjar* (referring to Moorish-style art created in Spain after the Reconquest) tower of the Iglesia de la Asunción whose flamboyant brick architecture evokes its Moorish past. The town's name derives from the Roman Compita-orum or 'point where paths cross': the earliest settlement was built beside one of the principle routes through the Almijara mountains and at a point where there was plentiful spring water.

The area's sheltered position, abundant sunshine and sub-tropical climate make the surrounding land ideal for cultivation. Olives, almonds and figs have been cultivated since Roman times while in recent times groves of avocado, kiwi and mango have all been added. But the village is best known for its *uvas pasas*

Ceramic panel next to the church

(sun-dried raisins) and its sweet moscatel wine. During its annual Noche del Vino festivity wine is handed out to one and all from a huge barrel set up in the Almijara square.

Many of Cómpeta's Moorish inhabitants, like those of nearby Frigiliana, chose to stay on after the Reconquest. They were to take part in the ill-fated *Morisco* (relating to the Moors who remained in Spain after the Reconquest) uprising of the 1570s which saw such a dramatic end on the high peak of El Fuerte (see Frigiliana section, Day 1). After a long period of prosperity the late 19th century would bring hard times for the village. The earthquake of 1884 caused huge destruction while the following year Cómpeta saw its population decimated by cholera.

After years of economic stagnation and large-scale emigration the village is now among the most prosperous of the eastern Axarquía. This is due in large part to the arrival of large numbers of foreign residents, attracted by the region's benign climate which blesses the village with an average of 320 days sunshine per year. The village has become a popular base for walking groups. Several great circuits begin in the village while the trailheads of routes leading to the top of La Maroma (2068m) are close to the village.

Cómpeta seen from the east

Recommended accommodation
Hotel Balcón de Cómpeta €€
www.hotel-competa.com
Friendly hotel with a pool and sea views, next to the start point of Day 3.

Salamandra Plaza B&B €–€€
www.salamandraplaza.com
Beautifully decorated B&B on the main square.

Recommended accommodation close to the village
Posada La Plaza €€
www.posada-laplaza.com
Comfortable small hotel in the pretty square of Canillas de Albaida.

Finca El Cerrillo €€–€€€
www.hotelfinca.com
Cosy, English-owned country house hotel on a high ridge above Canillas.

Contacts
Taxis: Máximo 657 506 954, Franquelo 620 267 615

DAY 3
Cómpeta to Sedella

Start	La Plaza de la Almijara, Cómpeta
Distance	14km
Ascent/Descent	575m/520m
Grade	Medium
Time	4hr 30min
Map	IGN 1:50000 Zafarraya 1040
Refreshments	In Canillas de Albaida early in the stage

The third leg of the Coast to Coast Walk leads you on through another beautiful slice of the Sierra de Almijara. The stage begins with a gentle stroll through the irrigated terraces that stretch west from Cómpeta past avocados, prickly pears, agaves and groves of olives and almonds. Passing through the pretty village of Canillas de Albaida you next descend to the Río Cájula whose leafy valley you follow north, close to the river.

Next comes a long climb across more open terrain to the high pass of Cruz del Muerto where vast vistas open out to the villages of the eastern and western Axarquía, to La Maroma's southern flank and south to the Mediterranean. Continuing along a broad forestry track that runs on west you finally descend to Sedella via a steep, zigzagging path to reach the village's tiny main square.

The stage begins in the main square of Cómpeta, La Plaza de la Almijara, next to the church. With your back to the church cross the square, climb a flight of steps then bear left along Calle San Antonio following a sign 'Juzgados de Cómpeta'. At the end of the street continue past Hotel Balcón de Cómpeta then a chapel dedicated to San Antonio. Follow the road for 40m as it swings right, then turn left at GR249 waymarking and go along a broad path which runs past a builder's yard. The path narrows and runs past towering agaves as Canillas de Albaida comes into view, running close to a water channel. After

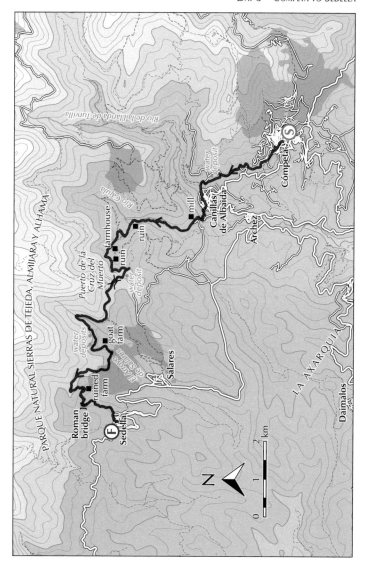

PARQUE NATURAL SIERRAS DE TEJEDA, ALMIJARA Y ALHAMA

Río de la llanda de Turvilla

water deposit

mill

Canillas de Albaida

Archez

Puerto de la Cruz del Muerto

Río Cájula

farmhouse

ruin

ruin

water deposit

goat farm

water deposits

Salares

El Arroyo de salares

LA AXARQUIA

Daimalos

ruined farm

Roman bridge

Sedella

F

S

Cómpeta

N

km

0   1   2

53

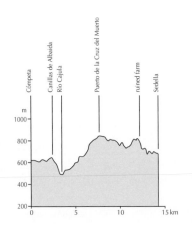

Looking west towards Canillas and La Maroma from the path close to Cómpeta

crossing a concreted drive the path reaches a tarmac road next to the gates to Villa Markez (**25min**).

Here bear right then after 300m turn left off the road at a cairn, picking up a narrow path which runs on

through groves of avocado and olives. It soon merges with a gravel track which, bearing right, meets the road you left earlier. Here turn left and descend past a **water deposit** to a four-way junction (**45min**).

Take the left fork, passing a spring to your left, and drop downhill to the left of the Capilla de Santa Ana. ▶ After 60m, as the road arcs left, head straight on past house no. 42 where a sign warns 'Cuidado con El Gato' ('Beware of the cat'). Take the second turning left into Calle Laberinto then after 10m cut right down a flight of steps along Calle Sierra Almijara which angles right then left to a junction in front of house no. 7. Here turn right then take the next left down Calle Alta which bears left then right to reach the main square of **Canillas** (**55min**).

It's worth diverting a few metres up to the chapel for a panoramic view of Canillas.

Leave the square at its western end along Calle Málaga then turn left down Calle Axarquía. At the end of the street bear right past house no. 16 then cut left past an electricity hut following GR249 waymarking to pick up a cobbled path which zigzags down towards the Cájula river.

Reaching the A-7207 turn right. After crossing the **Río Cájula** turn immediately right on a concrete track towards

The cobbled footpath leading down to the river below Canillas de Albaida

an old **mill**. Here the track divides. Ignoring a sign pointing right for 'Sendero' continue along the river's left bank, passing a signboard 'Río Cájula', via a path which crosses to and fro across the riverbed. The path, now running along the river's left bank, zigzags to a higher level before passing beneath two steep rock faces before descending and crossing the river once again.

After 200m you reach a fork. Here cut left through a gap in the oleander, cross the stream via stepping stones then climb steeply up the opposite bank. A fence now runs to your right. After 75m the path widens to become a track. Shortly before you reach a farm building and a sign 'Prohibido El Paso' branch right at a sign 'Camino Río/Sendero' along a narrow path that runs through a grove of young avocados. Passing the stumps of a line of poplars the path continues on its rather serpentine course, marked by cairns. At 300m beyond poplar stumps you cross over another path with a black plastic water pipe following its course. Bearing left the path winds down to the river which you again cross via stepping stones.

Following the path along the Cájula's east bank a **ruin** comes into sight on the opposite bank. Reaching a fork keep left, cross the Cájula a final time then follow a path that loops steeply upwards, passing right of the ruin. Adopting a northwesterly course the path climbs parallel to a tributary of the Cájula. Swinging right it crosses the streambed then bears right again and winds steeply up across terraced land to reach a broad dirt track.

Here, turning left, you pass just above a small **farmhouse**. After 175m the track loops left across a riverbed where there are two chestnut trees. Immediately beyond the river angle right up a narrow path which zigzags steeply up through an olive grove past a **ruin** with an old bread oven at one end. The path climbs steeply, crossing three *barrancos* (ravines) before reaching a forestry track where a sign 'Sendero' points back the way you've just come. Turning right you pass a fenced **water deposit**. Where the track arcs left turn right up a narrow path for 125m then, reaching the track once more, turn right again to reach a three-way junction at the **Puerto de la Cruz del Muerto** (924m) and a sign 'Parque Natural' (**2hr 25min**).

Leave the pass by bearing left: the track is now lined with cypress trees. Soon the track loops hard right: a deep gorge, **El Arroyo de Salares**, is now down to your left. Angling left the track crosses the barranco via a concrete bridge then runs on past a large **water deposit**. Sticking to the main track you pass by a ruined farm then a second **water deposit** with a tap (**3hr 20min**).

The track continues its descent, passing just above a **goat farm**. 50m beyond the farm cut right at a GR249 post up a narrower track which climbs past a house with a round tower. ▸ Reaching a fork bear right then after 150m, at a GR249 post, angle left away from the track to pick up a narrow path which climbs parallel to the edge of a water channel.

The path and channel level as you approach a group of pines. Just before the pines turn left and cross a streambed. Climbing to the top of a ridge you reach another marker post. Continue straight ahead, following the clearest path as you pass high above a **ruined farm** which you'll see down to your left. ▸

The path climbs to a ridgetop where you reach a cairn and a marker post. Here bear left to reach a flat grassy promontory then angle right along the ridgetop for 100m. Reaching a GR post angle hard left down an eroded path to the ruined farm you could see earlier. Pass behind the farm then head to the southern end of the terraces which lie just beneath it to reach another marker post and, to its left, a large cairn.

A few metres beyond the cairn you pick up a narrow path which runs down towards Sedella. Passing a small stone ruin it arcs right then, descending more steeply down a loose and eroded section, reaches the valley floor where you cross a **Roman bridge**. ▸

Beyond the bridge bear left and follow a track up to the village. Passing a goat farm you reach a sign 'Puente Romana 806m'. Here turn right. Climbing past house no. 17 take the next left to reach house no. 4. Here bear right then left to reach the main square of **Sedella** (**4hr 30min**).

Sedella soon comes into view.

It's possible to cut left down to the farm but it's easier to follow a clearer path which contours round the bowl of the valley, as described below.

The jury is out as to whether the bridge is Roman or dates from a later period.

SEDELLA (POPULATION 625, ALTITUDE 695M)

The village centre of Sedella

Lying just south of the valley where the sierras of Tejeda and Almijara run together, Sedella benefits from abundant spring waters that well up along the massif's southern flank and the shelter it provides against the cold, continental weather systems that come in from the north. South of the village the landscape is far less abrupt. Here, on meticulously terraced hillsides, vineyards and groves of olives and almonds have been planted since Roman times.

The first known reference to what came to be the village was in the 7th century when the Visigothic King Wamba asked his bishops to draw up a map of the area which included a settlement named Sedilla. The Moors called it Xedilla which reverted to Sedella after the Reconquest. A more fanciful explanation tells that the name originates in a comment by Queen Isabel La Católica who, referring to a battle close to the village, said 'Sé de ella', meaning 'Yes, I've heard about it'. The village's *Morisco* (relating to the Moors who remained in Spain after the Reconquest) population, encouraged by their militant *monfí* or clan leader, threw in their hand with the rebels during the uprisings of the late 16th century. Victory fell to the Christian armies but the legacy of Sedella's Islamic past is still visible in the village's plexus of narrow streets and in the *mudéjar* (referring to

Moorish-style art created in Spain after the Reconquest) brick tower of its Casa Torreón. As was the case with Cómpeta, the village suffered great damage in the 1884 earthquake which destroyed its parish church.

The reconstructed Iglesia de San Andrés makes for an interesting visit while on El Día de San Andrés, (17 January), a mass is held which begins with a blessing of the villagers' horses.

Sedella is now part of the Ruta del Mudéjar which links five of the region's villages whose architecture reflects their Moorish past.

Recommended accommodation close to the village
Lagabella €€
www.lagabella.com
Stylish B&B a few kilometres from Sedella. Owners offer pick-up from Sedella.

The House of Oranges €€
www.thehouseoforanges.com
English-run country B&B close to Salares. Can arrange pick-up in Sedella.

See also Cómpeta/Canillas de Albaida listings (Day 2) which are both a short taxi ride away.

Contacts
Ayuntamiento & Tourist Office: **www.sedella.es**
Taxi: nearest taxi in Canillas de Aceituno, Paco 658 905 446

La Iglesia de San Andrés

DAY 4
Sedella to Alcaucín

Start	La Plaza de la Constitución, Sedella
Distance	17.3km
Ascent/Descent	1050m/860m
Grade	Difficult
Time	6hr 40min
Map	IGN 1:50000 Zafarraya 1040
Refreshments	None en route
Advice	Parts of the path are overgrown on the middle section of the stage. Long trousers/gaiters will make for a more comfortable experience. Cloud can descend fast on La Maroma: having the GPX track as back-up could be reassuring here.

The Sedella to Alcaucín stage is among the most memorable sections of the Coast to Coast Walk, leading you up to a high footpath that hugs the spectacular, southern flank of La Maroma massif.

You're faced with a long, steep climb at the beginning of the stage following forestry tracks but your efforts are amply rewarded by a stunning middle section of trail where a snaking path leads past magnificent rock formations and two remote springs, the Pisadico and the Collado de la Gitana. Both springs make great spots for breaking the journey.

The footpath you follow during the latter part of the stage, which leads down to Alcaucín past the Collado del Pasaje, is overgrown in parts but is easy enough to follow.

The stage begins in front of the church in the main square of Sedella, La Plaza de la Constitución. With your back to the church cross the square and exit it along a 'No Entry' street. Just before reaching El Mesón de Frasco turn right and go up a cobbled footpath passing a sign 'Sendero Sedella-La Maroma' and GR249 waymarking.

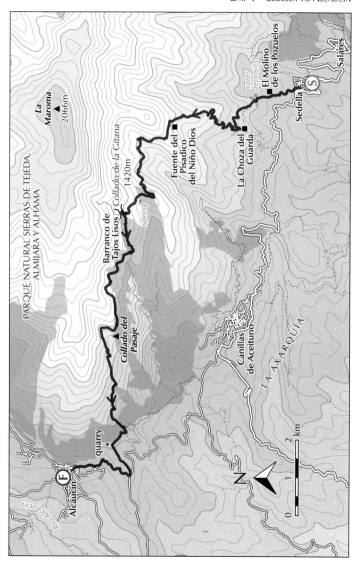

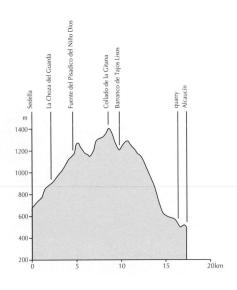

El Molino de los Pozuelos above Sedella

The path widens as it becomes concreted. Angling right it reverts to dirt track then narrows to become a

path which arcs round the edge of the terraced fields at the edge of the village before zigzagging more steeply upwards, cobbled in parts. The path crosses a water channel as it cuts through groves of almonds then runs up to a track in front of **El Molino de los Pozuelos** whose high water channel still feeds its millstones (**25min**).

Turn left. Go along the track for 50m then bear right and follow a track that loops steeply up past a fenced **water deposit** then a second group of white **water deposits**. Continuing straight ahead, ignoring GR249 waymarking pointing left, you pass a chain across the track as you climb gently, contouring round a deep ravine through a swathe of pine plantation. The track runs past a pole-roofed stone hut, **La Choza del Guarda**. 50m past the hut turn right, up another broad track.

After a steep climb, looping up through pine, cistus and broom, you reach a fork by a damaged marker post. Take the left track which soon passes an old threshing floor marked 'Era de Trillo'. Continuing to ascend, the track loops right as panoramic views open out to the south before reaching a flat area where forestry helicopters can land (**1hr 30min**).

On the northern side of this flat area are two footpaths. With your back to the sea ignore the right-hand path marked 'Sedella-La Maroma' but rather take a path that leads to the left: ahead you'll see the path arcing across the mountainside. Initially overgrown, the path passes an area of exposed rock before looping higher and resuming its previous course. Reaching a junction cut left for 40m to arrive at the **Fuente del Pisadico del Niño Dios**. Rejoin the path which now loops to a higher level then runs on across the mountainside, just left of a wire fence. Climbing more steeply it zigzags to the top of the ridge (**1hr 55min**).

From here the footpath you'll be following to the Collado de la Gitana is clearly visible. The path angles right, climbing slightly, then bearing left begins to descend as it contours round the bowl of the valley. This section is loose and steep in parts. The path crosses a streambed, climbs, then looping right traverses a second streambed. It climbs once more, crosses a rise, then descends to cross two more streambeds. The path, quite overgrown at this point, climbs across an area which has seen damage from a recent forest fire. Passing a *pozo de nieve* (snow pit) it leads to the top of the next divide where you reach a junction and a cairn. Here turn right (**2hr 55min**).

The path climbs, marked by cairns. Descending, you pass a marker post before crossing another ridge. Beyond the ridge the path contours round the saddle of another valley, shortly passing above another pozo de nieve then reaches a **spring**. ◄ Beyond the spring you reach more rocky, overgrown terrain: cairns help mark the way. The path, now cobbled in sections, runs up to the top of a rocky ridge. Cutting right for 75m you reach a breach in the rocks marked by twin cairns at the **Collado de la Gitana** pass (1420m) (**3hr 30min**). ◄

Just beyond the rise, descending for 10m, you reach a junction where a marker post points right. Ignore this (unless you fancy climbing La Maroma) and cut left down

The spring is easily missed lying just to the right of the path.

This is an excellent spot to rest with soaring views of Nerja, Cómpeta, Torrox and a huge swathe of the western Axarquía.

The south-facing slopes of La Maroma seen from close to the Collado de la Gitana

the footpath, roughly parallel to the ridge you've just crossed. The Viñuela reservoir comes into view. Reaching the bottom of the valley the path angles right towards the streambed at the upper end of the **Barranco de Tajos Lisos** where you reach a junction (**3hr 45min**).

Turn right then after 35m cross the oleander-lined streambed. As you contour gradually up round the *barranco* (ravine) the path becomes more overgrown. ▶ The path crosses a ridge then bears left into the next barranco where there's evidence of recent logging.

This is an area where ibex (*Capra pyrenaica hispanica*) can often be spotted.

After running fairly level the path begins to descend as views open out to the west: you can now see the path's continuation up ahead. The path bears right and descends as it contours round another deep gully. You soon cross a rocky streambed where there's a small water deposit (**4hr 50min**).

The path, invaded by rosemary, climbs again through thicker undergrowth. At times it's easier to drop off the path though care should be taken: parts are loose under-foot. After climbing steeply for a few metres the path resumes its descent, running down a ridge between two barrancos. Cairns help to guide you down. The path soon crosses another streambed by a solitary pine.

Ahead you now see the rocky outcrop of the **Collado del Pasaje**. Approximately 100m before reaching the outcrop angle right and continue your descent. The path becomes clearer but is loose in parts as it traverses more denuded terrain which has seen a forest fire in its recent past. Cairns and red dots mark the way. After following a ridge downwards the path loops right, crosses a stre-ambed, then runs down to the boundary fence of the Natural Park. Here angle left for 25m then go through a metal gate (**5hr 55min**).

Beyond the gate head for a gap between two pylons. Just beyond the second pylon, turning right, you pick up GR249 waymarking once again. Continue along a nar-row path which angles across the hillside back towards the fence through which you passed earlier. Crossing a streambed the path passes above a *calera* (pit where lime was made by firing limestone) then bears left to reach a white building next to a fenced **quarry**. Here turn left and follow a broad track which soon passes a white cottage. At the next flat-roofed building you reach a fork.

Keeping left you pass beneath transmitter masts then reach a junction. Here turn right towards Alcaucín. Soon you pass the quarry entrance. At the next fork, heading straight on, you pass beneath the village cemetery. Continue down into the village along Calle Calvario. At house no. 10 turn right to reach **Alcaucín** village square, La Plaza de la Constitución (**6hr 40min**).

ALCAUCÍN (POPULATION 2272, ALTITUDE 510M)

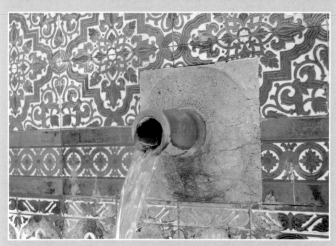

Detail of the Fuente de los Cinco Caños, Alcaucín

Alcaucín hugs the western slope of the Sierra Tejeda at the foot of the towering massif of La Maroma, 25 kilometres inland from the Mediterranean. The village lies beside one of the main passes through the mountains, leading north from Málaga through the Boquete de Zafarraya towards Granada. West of the village a fertile plain, irrigated by the spring waters from the sierra, stretches out towards Periana, Comares and the Viñuela reservoir, peppered with farmhouses and modern villas. This swathe of fertile land has long been a rich source of fruit and vegetables for Málaga.

The village's organic street plan reflects its Moorish origins, its name derived from the Arabic Al Cautin or 'gateway'. The ruins of the Moorish castle of Zalia lie close to the village. Phoenician remains discovered close to the castle revealed that the site has seen occupation for more than two millennia. During the *Morisco* (relating to the Moors who remained in Spain after the Reconquest), by which time the Moorish settlement lay abandoned, the castle was used to imprison rebel leaders.

The epicentre of the earthquake of Christmas Day 1884 was the Sierra Tejeda's western reaches when much of the village was razed to the ground. The earthquake coincided with unusually heavy snowfall in and around Alcaucín which was to hamper rescue operations.On the last day of October Alcaucín celebrates a festivity dedicated to the chestnut, which since medieval times has been cultivated on the lower reaches of the sierra. Other important local crops include almonds and olives: the valley to its west claims to produce the finest olive oil in Andalucía though countless Andalucían regions would lay similar claims.

Recommended accommodation
Hotel Sierra Tejeda €–€€
www.hotelsierratejeda.es
Comfortable and well-priced hotel a few metres from the end of Day 4.

Recommended accommodation close to the village
Hotel Rural Cortijo de Salia €€
www.cortijodesalia.com
Friendly rural hotel a few kilometres out of the village on the road to Ventas de Zafarraya.

Hotel La Viñuela €€€
www.hotelvinuela.com
Swish 4-star option a 15min drive from Alcaucín.

Contacts
Ayuntamiento: **www.ayuntamiento.es/alcauci**n
Taxi: Antonio 659 946 881, Carlos 629 760 075

DAY 5

Alcaucín to Ventas de Zafarraya

Start	La Plaza de la Constitución, Alcaucín
Distance	18.5km
Ascent/Descent	650m/250m
Grade	Medium/Difficult
Time	5hr 30min
Map	IGN 1:50000 Zafarraya 1040 & Colmenar 1039
Refreshments	None en route

Day 5 of the Coast to Coast Walk skirts round the northwestern flank of La Maroma massif past deep *barrancos* (ravines) before dropping down to Ventas de Zafarraya in a long, lazy loop. After a snaking footpath leads you up from the village most of the stage follows broad mountain tracks, allowing you to abandon yourself to the views out west and up to the pine-clad slopes of La Maroma.

This is one of the few sections of the Coast to Coast Walk where you loop away from your Atlantic-bound course, heading east for a few kilometres. This doubling back is amply rewarded by the astonishing variety of trees encountered in the vicinity of Cortijo de La Alcauca.

The nature of the terrain changes abruptly as you leave the final reaches of the Sierra de Almijara to drop down to the cultivated plain to the east of Ventas de Zafarraya. The village, which sees few visitors, has a couple of simple hostels and restaurants while its large population of migrant workers gives it a peculiarly North African flavour.

The arboretum at Cortijo de La Alcauca is a perfect picnic spot, coming some two-thirds into the stage.

The stage begins in the main square of Alcaucín, La Plaza de la Constitución, next to the town hall. With your back to the *ayuntamiento* (town hall) leave the square by cutting left and following a black railing upwards. Take the first right up Calle Arcos, passing house no. 2, then reaching a junction turn left along Calle Alta. At the end of the

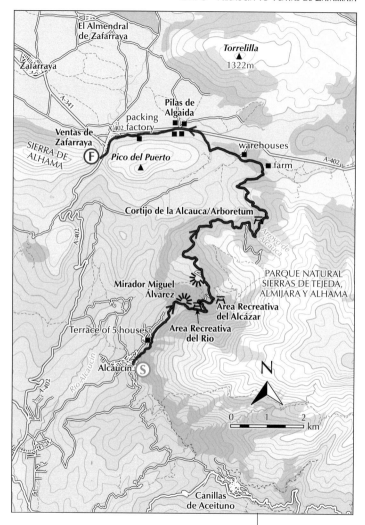

street turn right then bear left past a school along Calle
Carrión.

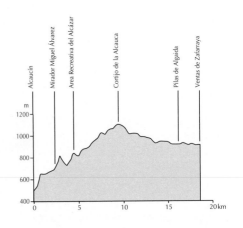

Reaching house no. 13 turn right and follow a sign 'Inicio Sendero' then passing left of a sign 'Sendero Alcaucín-Alcázar' follow a path that zigzags up through the pines before it adopts a northeasterly course as views open out to the west. Reaching a junction take the left path, maintaining your course, which soon merges with a wider one. The path passes through a metal gate then runs across a picnic area. On its far side it widens to become a track before it passes right of a terraced row of **five houses** then descends to merge with a broader track where you reach a sign 'Sierras de Tejeda, Almijara y Alhama'.

Bear right along the track which gradually climbs round the western reaches of La Maroma: bollards topped by wooden posts run to your left. The track loops right, now high above the barranco of the Río del Alcázar which is down to your left. Passing a damaged signboard marked 'Mirador del Pantano de Viñuela' it reaches the **Mirador Miguel Álvarez** and a statue of an ibex (**1hr 10min**). ◄ Following the track past the *mirador* (viewing point) you reach the **Área Recreativa El Río** where you pass the Cortijo del Alcázar restaurant.

There are stupendous views from the mirador out across the barranco.

Beyond the campsite the track passes left of a spring marked 'Fuente Eduardico' then loops left and resumes its ascent passing another damaged signboard for 'Mirador del Alcázar'. Soon you pass by a track off to the left signed 'Prohibido La Circulación de Vehículos a Motor'. Some 50m further up the main track cut right up a narrow path which climbs steeply up to the terraces beneath the **Área Recreativa del Alcázar**. Passing left of a run of barbecues climb a flight of steps, bear right then climb a second run of steps. Angling left you reach a sign describing the ascent of La Maroma and a car park. As you exit the car park two tracks angle left (**1hr 45min**).

Take the second of the tracks signed 'Mirador de Pedro Águila 1km' which immediately runs above five ceramic-topped tables. You shortly pass a turning to the left leading to the Mirador de Pedro Águila. Continue along the main track. ▶ The track continues to loop lazily round the mountain high above the Arroyo de Puente de Piedra. This is one of the few points on the Coast to Coast

Statue of ibex at Mirador Miguel Álvarez

The southern face of the Sierra de Alhama rises steeply up ahead of you, hiding your destination, Ventas de Zafarraya, from view.

71

The vegetation now begins to change as firs and junipers, and later cork oaks, put in an appearance.

Walk when you find yourself walking directly east, away from the Atlantic.

Angling right at a rocky outcrop you pass a signboard with a map of the Park. ◄

Soon you'll spot the terraced area and the ruined **Cortijo de La Alcauca** on the other side of the ravine of the Arroyo de la Alcauca. A final sharp loop brings you past the ruin and its picnic/recreational area (**3hr 10min**) accessed via a metal gate to the left of the track.

Looking west you now see the distant mountain ranges you'll be traversing later on the Coast to Coast Walk.

Exiting the picnic area via a flight of steps rejoin the track which runs on through an area where there is an **arboretum** down to your left, gradually descending towards the plain stretching east from Ventas de Zafarraya. ◄

The track angles left then climbs between fences before descending once again past a large water tank with several exit pipes (**3hr 55 min**). Here the track loops left then passes above a **farm**.

The arboretum at Cortijo de La Alcauca

Just beyond the farm you see the first GR7 marker post encountered on the stage as you merge with a

broader track which runs past the **warehouses** of a crate manufacturer then reaches a four-way junction. Here a sign 'Zona de Acampada La Alcauca' points back the way you've just come.

Isolated farm beyond La Alcauca

Here head straight ahead up a rough track, passing a drain with a blue metal cover. GR7 posts mark your way. The track climbs, passing between two farm sheds before passing left of a metal-roofed water deposit. Passing left of a large breeze-block building next to a pylon, after 300m it reaches a junction with another track. Turn right and follow a narrower track over a low rise then down towards the plain stretching out from Ventas de Zafarraya. Bearing left you pass a drinking trough then a farm shed before cutting across flatter land to reach the road next to the large warehouse. Angling left along the road continue through the linear hamlet of **Pilas de Algaida**. A few metres beyond the restaurant and Pensión Al Andalus cut left at a damaged GR7 sign for 'Ventas de Zafarraya, 2km' along a dirt track which angles away from the road.

After 1km you pass between the warehouses of a **packing factory**. Passing right of a 5-a-side football pitch you reach a junction. Turn left, pass a 'No Entry' sign,

You're at the provincial boundary between Granada and Málaga at the pass known as the Boquete de Zafarraya. From the *mirador* there's a superb panoramic view of the mountains of Axarquía.

then angle right past what were once the station buildings of Ventas de Zafarraya. At the end of the street pass left along Calle Estación. At the next junction head straight on following the course of the old, narrow gauge railway track. Passing a large warehouse the tarmac surface of the old track reverts to dirt then crosses a bridge over the **A-402** before reaching a mirador with a ceramic map of the villages and mountains which lie before you (**5hr 30min**). ◄

The village of **Ventas de Zafarraya** is immediately to your right.

VENTAS DE ZAFARRAYA, GRANADA (POPULATION 1308, ALTITUDE 906M)

The area surrounding Ventas de Zafarraya has seen settlement since prehistoric times: a number of Palaeolithic remains have recently been discovered on the hillsides just south of the town near to Boquete de Zafarraya, including the jawbone of one of our Neanderthal ancestors. Bronze Age implements have also been discovered while Visgothic remains were found within the present urban nucleus. During the Moorish period the fertile plain surrounding the present settlement came under the sway of different Taifa kingdoms who vied for its bountiful produce.

The 1884 earthquake had the same catastrophic effect on the village as it did in many others in the region with 80% of its houses destroyed and more than 70 villagers losing their lives. Funds were sent back from the Spanish colony in Cuba for the village's reconstruction and for many years it was known as Nueva Habana.

The present-day settlement expanded along the edge of the cog railway line which was built up through the Boquete in order to transport produce from the plain, known then as La Dehesa, down to Málaga. Completed in 1922 the railway ushered in an era of prosperity for local farmers who could now transport the produce of their smallholdings quickly to the capital. The trip up through the Boquete on the cog railway became a popular excursion for wealthy Malagueños and a hotel was built close to the station. The train made its final journey in 1960 by which time motorised transport had become a more viable means of moving merchandise.

Nowadays the village sees few tourists apart from walkers following the southern variant of the GR7 footpath with which the Coast to Coast Walk overlaps at this stage. Most of the low-paid work in the surrounding fields and packing houses is carried out by migrant workers from the Maghreb and some shops and bars in the village have a distinctly North African feel.

The surrounding plain is still intensively farmed and specialises in early and late fruit and vegetables. It's difficult to imagine that in medieval times this same plain was covered in *dehesa* (forest which has been partially cleared to leave selected species of cork and holm oaks), at which time it was renowned for the quality of its acorn-reared pigs. Much of this forest was felled in the 16th and 17th century for ship building.

Recommended accommodation
Aquí Te Quiero Ver €
958 362 222
Basic but highly recommended pensión a few metres away from the end of Day 5.

Recommended accommodation close to the village
Restaurante Al Andalus €
958 362 139
Friendly restaurant with 3 simple en suite rooms that you pass towards the end of Day 5.

Hotel Rural Cortijo de Salia €€
See Alcaucín section (Day 4).

Contacts
Ayuntamiento: **www.ventasdezafarraya.es**
Taxi: nearest taxis in Alcaucín, Antonio 659 946 881, Carlos 629 760 075

The fertile plain to the east of Ventas de Zafarraya

DAY 6
Ventas de Zafarraya to Riogordo

Start	The mirador beside the old railway line at Boquete de Zafarraya on the south side of Ventas de Zafarraya
Distance	23.4km
Ascent/Descent	345m/865m
Grade	Medium/Difficult
Time	6hr 30min
Map	IGN 1:50000 Zafarraya 1040 & Colmenar 1039
Refreshments	Bars in Guaro and Pulgarín Alto

This longish leg of the Coast to Coast Walk leads down to Riogordo across the southern flank of the Sierra de Alhama. The first section of the walk follows the course of the old railway line that once connected Ventas de Zafarraya and Málaga (see Ventas de Zafarraya section, Day 5).

Passing through Guaro you pick up the old drovers' path that leads from Málaga to Granada. At this stage you're following a section of the southern branch of the GR7 and the GR249. After looping round the flank of the Sierra de Enmedio there's a steep climb to the top of the Puerto de Sabar before you gently descend to Riogordo along a leafy track.

Highlights of the stage include outstanding views of La Axarquía and the Mediterranean, groves of ancient olive trees and the source of the Río Guaro.

The stage begins at the **mirador** beside the old railway line at the Boquete de Zafarraya pass, next to a damaged ceramic map. From the mirador head away from Ventas de Zafarraya along the railway line in a southwesterly direction. After approximately 250m the track runs through a **tunnel**. Passing ruined buildings to your right and left you reach a faded sign on a rock pointing left to 'Aldea Rural El Cañuelo'. Ignore this sign and continue along the old railway line.

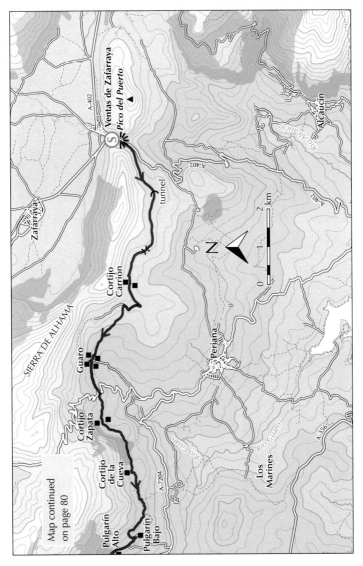

Map continued
on page 80

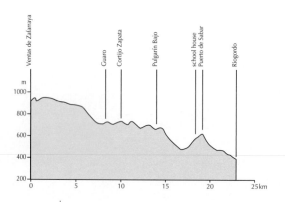

To your left the hilltop village of Comares comes into view along with the Viñuela reservoir and there are fine vistas back towards the towering massif of La Maroma.

Passing beneath a **bridge** (**1hr 10min**) the track runs past the farm buildings of **Cortijo Carrión** then passes above a house to the left of the old track. ◄ Lined by ancient pine trees the track runs up to a junction (**1hr 40min**).

Here turn right, leaving the old railway line, following signs for 'Guaro' and 'Marchamona' and GR7/GR249 waymarking. The track loops hard right then runs up to another junction. Here take the left fork signposted 'Aldea de Guaro' and follow a steep dirt track down to the hamlet of **Guaro** where you reach a junction with a concrete-surfaced road. Here bear slightly left following a sign 'Pulgarín Alto' and head on through the village.

Reaching a junction next to the village post boxes you could cut right to reach the point where the Río Guaro rises. Otherwise, continue past the Caserón de Guaro restaurant. Reaching a group of houses you pass a bench to the left of the road where there's a spring and shade beneath a stand of coppiced poplars. Beyond the spring the track meets a road by a 'Stop' sign (**2hr 35min**).

You can replenish your water at the spring just beneath the farmhouse.

Head straight across the road to pick up a broad track, signposted 'Cortijo Zapata'. ▶ The track runs across an *era* (threshing floor) then descends through a swathe of olive groves, crosses a bridge then passes just above **Cortijo Zapata**. Adopting an uphill course it becomes concreted then passes between a shed made of breeze blocks and a water deposit. Reaching a fork at the top of the rise continue along the main track, signed with GR249 waymarking, passing through a swathe of *monte bajo* (low-growing forest typical of parts of La Axarquía) on the southern flank of the Sierra de Enmedio. After ascending for a short distance the track levels then descends. Running down through olive groves it arcs left before passing between the buildings of **Cortijo de la Cueva** (**3hr 30min**).

Some 30m beyond the farm you reach a junction and a GR sign for 'Riogordo, 5hrs'. Here, turning right along a dirt track, you cross the farm's era. The track runs on westwards, passing four identical galvanised metal gates, leading to olive groves to its left. At a set of blue

You're now following the old drovers' path that connected Málaga with Granada.

Heading west towards the Sierra de Enmedio

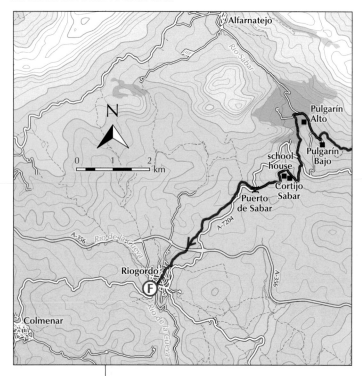

metal gates the track arcs right, descends past a group of ancient olives. then reaches a fork. Branching left, still following GR249 posts, you drop down to reach a concreted track. Here bear right and continue your descent. The track runs past a palm-filled garden then, passing by the hamlet of **Pulgarín Bajo**, reaches the MA-157 (**4hr**).

Turn right and go along the road till you reach the hamlet of **Pulgarín Alto** and a restaurant signed with the same name. Continue along the MA-157 which runs past a transmitter mast then a farm signed Cortijo Molina. A few metres past the farm branch left at signs for 'Bolaños' and 'Tajo del Gomer'. Descending steeply you pass a spring. Some 150m past the spring branch left at GR waymarking down a steep dirt track through groves of olive. Crossing a streambed the track levels before descending once more. ▸

The track runs past a house with a tall palm tree then, looping right, reaches the A-7204.

Turn left and follow the road for 150m then cut right at a sign for 'Venta Pepe Alba' along a dirt track. After 75m the track angles right, runs steeply downhill, then passes between two farmhouses. Sticking to your same course you pass a small breeze-block building then reach a fork. Here angle right down an overgrown path which arcs right towards a rusting metal sign. Bearing sharply left for 15m cross a streambed via stepping stones. ▸

Angling right beyond the stream you reach a broad farm track. Turn right here and follow the track up past cattle and dog pens to reach **Cortijo Sabar**. Descending for 75m beyond the farm you reach a junction with a tarmac road (**4hr 50min**).

Turn left and continue past an old **school house**, topped by a belfry and a cross. After 150m the track, concreted, bears left, crosses a streambed then arcs right and climbs, parallel to a line of pylons. Reaching a junction by a pylon turn right, sticking to the concreted track. After levelling the track climbs once more, passing above a house backed by six cypress trees. Continuing past a second house you reach the **A-7204** (**5hr 25min**) a few metres before it cuts through the Puerto de Sabar. Angle left across the road then, following GR249 waymarking, continue up a dirt track. Following a ridgetop you're treated to a vast panoramic view of the mountains to your north.

After descending you reach a junction where GR249 waymarking points right. Here cut left, passing a GR 'X' marker post, and continue down a quiet lane towards Riogordo, passing a number of villas. Reaching recycling bins and a junction, keep right, and continue down an agave-lined dirt track. The track levels then crosses the stream of Arroyo de las Morenas then continues its descent before it passes beneath the A-356. Running on past twin gates topped by olive millstones you reach the

Looking south you can now see the steep track you'll later be following up to the Puerto de Sabar.

If you approach the stream quietly you may spot Spanish pond turtles, *Mauremys leprosa*.

Poppies beneath the olives en route to Riogordo

first houses of **Riogordo**. Passing beneath a cemetery you reach a junction with a tarmac road (**6hr 15min**).

Head straight on, immediately passing house no. 118. The road arcs right as it runs beneath a small park then reaches a junction. Here turn left down Calle Málaga. At the bottom of the street head straight across at a junction. At the next junction bear right across Plaza de la Fuente Nueva then angle left down a one-way street to reach the Plaza de la Constitución (**6hr 30min**).

RIOGORDO (POPULATION 2812, ALTITUDE 389M)

Riogordo fans out around a deep depression which was hollowed out over the millennia between the Sierra de Caramolos and the Sierra de los Montes by the Río de la Cueva. Phoenicians and Romans established settlements close to the village, attracted by abundant artesian waters to both north and south and a sizeable settlement was to grow up during the Islamic period.

Finally ceded to the Catholic monarchs in 1487 just five years before the rendition of Granada, Riogordo had seen almost nine centuries of occupation by

Riogordo and the tower of Nuestra Señora de Gracia

the Moors. They called it Majianza and the present village, with its narrow streets of whitewashed buildings, bears the stamp of its North African roots. According to some sources the rebel chieftain Omar Ben Hafsun (see Bobastro section, Day 10) was born in the Castillo de Aute, originally a Visgothic fortress, which lies in ruins just outside the town.

The village gained considerable renown thanks to the resistance it offered to the French forces during the Guerra de la Independencía in the early 19th century. The villagers, led by the priest of the village who adopted a new role as captain of cavalry, inflicted heavy casualties on the Napoleonic forces before reinforcements arrived from Granada and the French took their revenge. The village later gained a degree of notoriety thanks to the large numbers of bandits who worked the mountain passes leading south through the mountains: the tortured nature of the terrain offered many a safe bolt-hole.

An unusual feature of the village is a number of small niches built into the fabric of its houses. They contain images of Christ, saints and the Virgin and mostly date from the 16th century. The village is unique in celebrating an annual Día del Caracol (the last Sunday in May) when snails gathered in the surrounding hills are served up al caldillo (in a rich sauce) in the main square. Riogordo's Holy Week celebrations on Good Friday and the following Saturday, when villagers re-enact the Passion, have recently been declared Fiestas de Interés Turístico Nacional.

Recommended accommodation
Restaurante La Era €
www.hostalmesonlaera.es
Comfortable rooms, good food and low prices. Close to the end point of Day 6.

Recommended accommodation close to the village
Hotel Balcón de los Montes €€
www.balcondelosmontes.es
Friendly small hotel with great views at the edge of El Colmenar, 6km from Riogordo.

Hotel Restaurante Belén €
www.hotelrestaurantebelen.com
Simple hotel at the top end of El Colmenar, 6km from Riogordo

Casa Algarrobo €€
www.logereninandalusie.com
Dutch-run farm hotel on a high hilltop, 15min by car from Riogordo.

Contacts
Ayuntamiento: **www.riogordo.es**
Taxi: nearest taxi is in El Colmenar at 6km, Pepe 625 836 089

La Plaza de la Constitución and Riogordo's oldest public water taps

DAY 7

Riogordo to Villanueva de Cauche

Start	La Plaza de la Constitución, Riogordo
Distance	16.3km
Ascent/Descent	710m/410m
Grade	Medium/Difficult
Time	4hr 45min
Map	IGN 1:50000 Colmenar 1039
Refreshments	None en route

The seventh leg of the Coast to Coast Walk follows farm tracks and quiet country roads westwards to the tiny village of Villanueva de Cauche.

The day begins with a steep climb through olive groves to the top of a high ridge north of El Colmenar. Arriving at the hamlet of Cortijo los Moriscos you pick up the Cañada Real de Alhama a Antequera, the old drovers' way, which leads down across open farmland to the Río de Guadalmedina.

From here you're faced with the second steep climb of the day as you head up towards the southern flank of the Sierra de Caramolos. As you ascend, mesmerising views open out to all points of the compass. You then follow a quiet road to the day's highest point from where you descend for 4km to the tiny village of Villanueva de Cauche.

Although this leg includes one of the two sections of road walking of the Coast to Coast Walk you can expect little passing traffic, especially if you walk the final hour or so between 2pm and 3pm when most of Andalucía is at lunch.

The stage begins in front of the *ayuntamiento* (town hall) in the main square of Riogordo, La Plaza de la Constitución. With your back to the town hall turn left and exit the square along Calle Real passing by the church of Nuestro Padre Jesús Nazareño. Reaching a building marked Casa del Pueblo turn right. After passing a row of recycling bins turn left and cross a **bridge** over the Río de la Cueva.

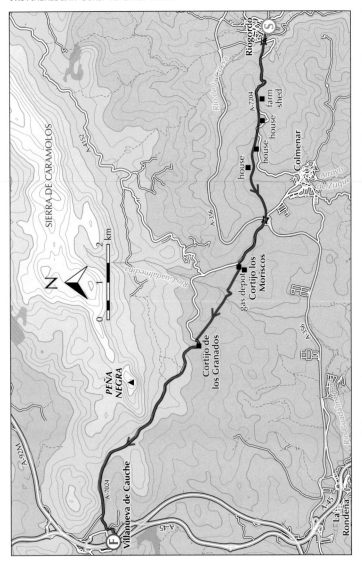

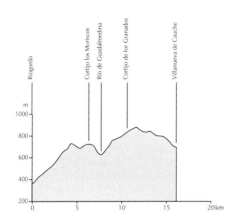

At 10m beyond the bridge bear right, away from the tarmac, and climb an indistinct dirt track across an open

Olive grove backed by the Sierra de Caramolos

87

field. After running along the lower edge of a grove of olives it reaches the A-7204 by a chevron. Bear right along the road which loops upwards before levelling as you pass to the right of a **farm shed**. Where the road arcs left angle right, away from the tarmac, following a sign Ruta La Molina along a gravel-surfaced track which climbs steeply through groves of olives. The track levels then passes a **house** before it meets once more with the A-7204.

Continue along the road for 40m then turn right then immediately left and continue up a track which passes just to the right of a set of black metal gates then a line of poplars. ◄ Bearing right the track levels as it passes just right of a **house** flanked by two cylindrical water deposits before reaching a four-way junction. Here maintain your course following a second sign for Ruta La Molina.

As you climb steeply upwards views open out to the north towards the Sierra de Camarolos.

The track continues to ascend steeply. Levelling then descending for a short distance it runs past a **house** topped by a satellite dish before reaching another four-way junction. Here continue straight ahead, passing just right of a sign for Zona de Reserva. The track resumes its uphill course as El Colmenar comes into sight to your left. As it levels you reach another junction.

Here turn right then after 5m turn left, resuming your former course. After descending, the track angles left towards the A-7204. Some 25m before it reaches the road turn right and follow a less distinct track for 40m to reach the MA-7204 just before a **bridge** spanning the A-356. Cross the bridge and continue along the MA-7204 following signs for Alfarnate and Alfarnatejo. After 1.4km you reach the hamlet of **Cortijo los Moriscos** (**1hr 50min**).

Here, immediately past Hotel Casona los Moriscos, just before reaching Venta los Moriscos, turn left and follow a farm track to reach a **gas depot** surrounded by a breeze-block wall. Follow the track for 5m as it bears right then turn left, following painted arrows on the breeze-block wall, and drop down a steep, dirt track. Crossing a streambed the track bears left as it passes beneath a tractor shed. A fence now runs to your right.

Reaching the valley floor the track arcs left for 60m then back right before crossing the streambed of **Río de Guadalmedina** beyond which it runs up to a junction with a more clearly defined track.

Here, turning right, after 50m you each a pylon. Continue past the pylon for 10m then turn left and follow a strip of unploughed land up between open fields. Climbing steeply you pass a number of metal Coto signs. Reaching the top of the first field to your right, maintain your course along the left side of the next field, now following a faint track. As the track begins to level you pass to the right of a pile of painted white rocks. The track becomes clearer as it passes to the left of a fenced olive grove straddling a low hilltop.

> Sweeping **views** open out to all four points of the compass. La Maroma is visible to the east and the coastal mountain ranges to the south, while out west the toothed ridgeline of El Torcal comes into view and, beyond, the higher reaches of La Sierra de las Nieves.

The track runs on towards the southern flank of the **Sierra de Caramolos** and the sheer cliff face of Peña Negra. Passing a Coto sign the track merges with a better-surfaced track. Maintaining your course continue past a small white house, the **Cortijo de los Granados**. Passing a pylon you reach the A-7204 (**3hr 15min**).

Turn left and follow the road. You'll be following the tarmac for 6km but will encounter little passing traffic.

A few metres beyond the km37 post you reach the top of a pass and the highest point of the stage at 883m. From here the road descends, passing a (dry) spring to its right then a farm with two palm trees. ▶

At this point it's possible to hop over the crash barrier to your left and walk along sections of the old road.

Reaching a junction turn left to follow a sign for Villanueva de Cauche. After 40m bear right, descend past a faded GR7 sign to the edge of the village, then take the second road to the right, Calle Granada, to reach the village's sleepy square between a fountain and the church of **Villanueva de Cauche** (**4hr 45min**).

*Approaching
Villanueva de Cauche
from the east*

VILLANUEVA DE CAUCHE (POPULATION 65, ALTITUDE 694M)

Hugging a ridgetop to one side of the A-45 motorway, close to the top of the Puerto de las Pedrizas, Villanueva de Cauche sees little in the way of passing trade. A five-minute walk around the village will suffice to get you acquainted with its half dozen streets of whitewashed houses.

Home to just 65 inhabitants – the municipality numbers more like 300 – at the end of the 19th century its population was almost three times that of today, at a time when most villagers were working the lands of the surrounding estate. This was the last village in Spain to have officially been owned by a local grandee, the Marquis of Cauche, who was given title of his lands in the 17th century. He built the terraced houses for his minions who paid him tithe with the produce of their vegetable gardens and the eggs of their chickens.

The physiognomy of Villanueva de Cauche has changed very little and its sleepy village centre, with its fountain, church tower and starkly Andaluz architecture, has been used on a number of occasions for filming when a period setting is required. The village has one tiny bar which doubles as a shop, along with

The church in Villanueva de Cauche's tiny square

a small roadside hotel (found a few hundred metres beyond the village, reached by following the first 15 minutes of Day 8).

Villanueva de Cauche marks the point at which the GR7 footpath (Tarifa to Athens) divides into its northern and southern Andalucían variants.

Recommended accommodation
Hotel Las Pedrizas €
952 730 850
Simple roadside hotel close to the motorway with good home cooking, a 15min walk from the finish of Day 7.

Recommended accommodation close to the village
Hotel La Sierra €€
www.hotellasierra.com
Comfortable roadside hotel, a 5min drive north of Villanueva de Cauche.

Contacts
Ayuntamiento: **www.antequera.es**
Taxi: nearest taxis in Villanueva de la Concepción, Miguel 670 766 787 or in El Colmenar, Pepe 625 836 089

DAY 8

Villanueva de Cauche to Villanueva de la Concepción

Start	In front of the church, Villanueva de Cauche
Distance	15km
Ascent/Descent	390m/490m
Grade	Medium
Time	4hr 30min
Map	IGN 1:50000 Colmenar 1039 & Ardales 1038
Refreshments	Restaurant/bar next to the motorway 15min into the walk
Advice	Pack long trousers or gaiters in your pack for the slightly overgrown section beyond Puente de Garrayo.

This is one of the shorter sections of the Coast to Coast Walk yet it still makes for a fine day of hiking. After passing beneath the A-45 motorway that cuts south towards Málaga you climb across open fields beneath the rugged flank of the Sierra de las Cabras, following the old drovers' path of La Cañada Real de la Fuente de los Remedios a Colmenar.

Angling back to the southwest you pick up another stunning section of the *cañada real* (a drovers' path, created by royal decree, for the passage of livestock) that once led from Málaga to Madrid. This ancient cart track is lost at the point where you pass beneath Cortijo de Garrayo. It's here that you reach the Puente de Garrayo which appears like a phantom from another age in the midst of a vast field of wheat.

Beyond the bridge the old drovers' path becomes clearer as it runs southwest towards Villanueva de la Concepción before crossing the extraordinary Puente del Paraíso. Passing a number of small farms views open out to the deeply weathered karst formations of El Torcal before a narrow footpath leads you up to Villanueva.

If you've spent the night in Hotel Las Pedrizas pick up these notes at 15min.

The stage begins in front of the church in the tiny village of Villanueva de Cauche next to a fountain. ◄ With your back to the church exit the square by heading east along Calle Granada. At the end of the street turn left then bear

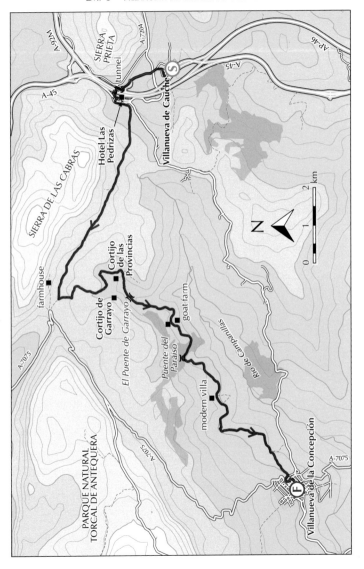

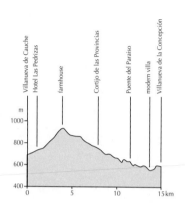

left again and climb up past a GR7 marker post to a junction with the A-7204. Head straight across following a sign 'A92M Granada'.

Passing the gates of a modern house with a sign 'La Era de Rodrigo' follow a line of eucalyptus trees parallel to the eastern side of the A-45 motorway. Reaching a roundabout head straight across. After 150m, reaching a junction, turn left past a GR7 sign. ◄ Continue along a stony track which arcs right then left then passes beneath the A45 via a long **tunnel**.

The junction marks the point where the GR7 northern and southern variants meet (or divide if you are approaching from the west).

At the end of the tunnel the track reaches a tarmac road. Turn left and head down to the entrance to **Hotel Las Pedrizas (15min)**. Here turn right and go through another tunnel. As you exit the tunnel bear left following a sign for 'Málaga, Granada, Córdoba, Sevilla'. Follow the road and a crash barrier for a few metres then turn right along a broad farm track which soon arcs right as it climbs away from the motorway across open fields, parallel to the southwestern flank of the Sierra de las Cabras. Reaching the top of a first rise you come to a fork. Here, heading straight ahead, Villanueva de la Concepción soon comes into view.

After a long climb the track levels then descends as the jagged ridgeline of El Torcal comes into sight, up ahead to your left. Passing beneath a **farmhouse** the track runs past two GR7 marker posts then reaches a junction with a track running up from the southwest (**1hr 50min**).

Here turn sharply left, almost doubling back on your previous course, and follow a broad track down into the valley. ▶ Looping down into the valley the track passes by the metal entrance gates to **Cortijo de Garrayo** marked 'Propiedad Privada: Prohibido El Paso'. Just past the gates the track bears left then once more right. Crossing a streambed you pass by the track that leads down to the **Cortijo de las Provincias** which is normally closed off with a metal chain. Stick to the main track which after 50m runs past a second track cutting in towards the farm. After 30m the track crosses a streambed.

At 10m beyond the streambed turn right off the track and follow a faint tractor track down the edge of a field, some 30m to the left bank of the streambed. After holding your course past a small water deposit the track becomes clearer as you come to a bridge, **El Puente de Garrayo**,

You're now following the old cañada real which led from Málaga to Madrid.

The descent towards Cortijo de Garrayo

looking somewhat surreal in the midst of the surrounding field. Passing by an equally incongruous-looking information board, cross the bridge (**2hr 50min**).

Continue along the top of the field by way of an indistinct track which, overgrown in parts, runs parallel to a fence which is to your right. It soon improves, running on in a southwesterly direction.

The track becomes more clearly defined, its original cobbling visible in parts. After running beneath a horse stable the track passes between the buildings of a **goat farm** then runs on between fences as El Torcal comes into view once again. You reach a junction where a concreted track angles hard down to the left: ignore this and stick to your same course. Passing a ruin the track crosses the **Puente del Paraiso**, an impressive piece of 18th-century engineering (**3hr 10min**).

Beyond the bridge the track arcs left, runs steeply uphill, then passes another farm with an old *era* (threshing floor) to one side. Descending, Villanueva de la Concepción again comes into view as the track passes another farm with green, metal-roofed sheds. Some 50m past the farm, at the point where the track loops hard left, its surface now concreted, you reach a pylon with a yellow cross on one of its struts. Here two tracks cut into the right. Turn right and go along the lower of the tracks then continue round the mountainside on roughly the same course that you were previously following.

The track passes beneath a manicured **modern villa** with palm trees and a Moorish-looking tower before running up to twin galvanised metal gates which lead to a small house to your left. Passing right of the gates the track becomes less distinct. Running past a pylon and a water tank it becomes cobbled then passes by a fenced enclosure (**3hr 40min**).

Bearing right the track cuts between a ruin and a small white building with a circular window on its eastern side before bearing back left and resuming its previous course. Crossing a streambed it runs on between groves of olives and almonds before reaching more open countryside. ◄ Running past another fenced building the

The crenellated ridgeline of El Torcal is again visible to your right.

track crosses a streambed beyond which you pass a wall made of huge boulders. Crossing a second streambed the track bears hard left.

Here turn right up a narrow path which climbs between two fields. Initially indistinct, the path becomes clearer then crosses a streambed. Beyond the streambed maintain your course across the next field. The path improves, now running just left of a wooden-posted fence. After passing a ramshackle shed it merges with a track which leads up to the first houses of Villanueva where you come to a junction. Turning right and climbing steeply you reach the **A-7075**.

Turn left, head down past the *ayuntamiento* (town hall) then reaching the next junction turn left again and cross a pedestrian crossing. Continue downhill then take the third turning right along Calle Real to reach the village's main square, La Plaza de Andalucía (**4hr 30min**).

Approaching Villanueva de la Concepción

VILLANUEVA DE LA CONCEPCIÓN (POPULATION 3383, ALTITUDE 595M)

Fountain in the square of García Caparros, Villanueva de la Concepción

Villanueva de la Concepción – it takes its name from its patron La Virgen de la Inmaculada Concepción – lies in the lee of the craggy massif of El Torcal, one of the largest swathes of karst limestone in Europe. With a boundary of 17 kilometres and numerous marked routes snaking their way through a fantasia of deeply weathered rock the Torcal Natural Park draws in thousands of visitors every year. An early section of Day 9 of the Coast to Coast Walk runs just beneath its southern edge where the jagged ridgeline gives an idea of what lies within the park. It's worth slotting in a quick visit, possibly in the afternoon by taxi after the shortish leg from Villanueva de Cauche.

South of Villanueva the landscape changes abruptly as rocky outcrops give way to rolling groves of olives and almonds, and fields of wheat and barley. This area was previously known as Los Campos de Cámara and was an important source of agricultural produce for Málaga. One of the major cañadas reales from the city through the mountains to Madrid passed just east of the town. You follow a section of this ancient cart track on Day 8 when you cross two of its most impressive bridges.

Nowadays the village economy is based on agriculture and small businesses with a number of workshops manufacturing women's clothing on piece rates for textile companies in northern Spain. Unemployment is high since the advent of the current recession when many workers returned from the building sites of the Costa del Sol.

Like all Andalucían villages Villanueva is big on fiestas. Carnival celebrations are fêted with great gusto for three days: the August *feria* (fair) is a bacchanalian romp while its Fiesta de los Verdiales, which takes place on the last Saturday in July, is among the oldest summertime parties in Málaga and has recently been given the accolade of Fiesta de Interés Turístico Nacional.

Recommended accommodation
El Rincón del Torcal €€
www.rincondeltorcal.com
Spruce village B&B close to the end point of Day 8 and to bars and restaurants.

Recommended accommodation close to the village
Hotel La Posada del Torcal €€€
www.torcalboutiquehotel.com
Swish lodging a few kilometres northwest of Villanueva with a pool and great food.

If Villanueva listings are full or beyond budget Antequera, a 15min drive away, has several less expensive places to stay including:

Hotel Coso Viejo €–€€
www.hotelcosoviejo.es
Characterful hotel at the heart of the old town with a fabulous restaurant next door.

Hospedería Colon €
www.castelcolon.com
Excellent 2-star hostelry at the heart of the old town.

Contacts
Ayuntamiento: www.villanuevaconcepcion.es
Taxi: Miguel 670 766 787

Villanueva seen from the south backed by the ridgeline of El Torcal

DAY 9

*Villanueva de la Concepción to
Valle de Abdalajís*

Start	La Plaza de Andalucía, Villanueva de la Concepción
Distance	21.3km
Ascent/Descent	490m/650m
Grade	Medium/Difficult
Time	6hr
Map	IGN 1:50000 Ardales 1038
Refreshments	None en route

The ninth leg of the Coast to Coast Walk begins with a steep climb up from Villanueva towards the Sierra del Torcal. After running west beneath El Torcal's jagged limestone ridge you later angle north to pick up a section of the ancient drovers' path which joined Málaga with Antequera.

After a long climb towards the Sierra de Chimenea the route runs westwards once again along a more level section of track to reach La Fuente de la Higuera. From here there are soaring views south across La Axarquía and on to the Mediterranean.

After a short section of tarmac road you continue along a little-used farm track that leads down past a number of isolated farms to the pretty village of Valle de Abdalajís.

The stage begins at the bottom of the Plaza de Andalucía next to a bank. With your back to the bank head uphill past an ornamental fountain then exit the square along Callejón del Viento. Take the second turning left, continue past the church of La Inmaculada Concepción, then take the next turning right and climb Calle Fresca. At the end of the street head up a flight of steps, cross a pedestrian crossing then continue up following a sign for 'Colegio Público Ciudad de Oscua'.

The road, **El Carril del Agua**, climbs steeply past a group of houses and a college of secondary

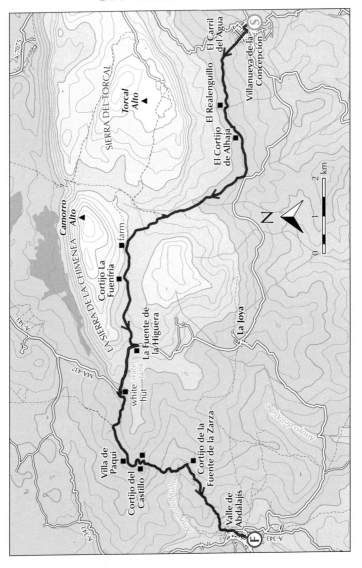

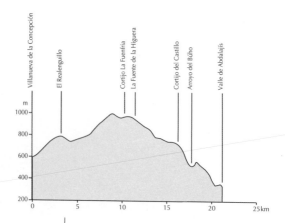

education. ◄ The road narrows as you climb towards the southern flank of the Sierra del Torcal, soon passing gates marked 'El Cappel'.

Arcing left the track levels as it runs past a small house with a neo-classical balustrade. Reaching a fork in the track keep left, sticking to the main track, which now

Waymarking indicates that you're now on one of the southern variants of the Camino de Santiago.

El Torcal seen from the west

adopts a westerly course. The asphalt of the track reverts to concrete and then to dirt as you continue to contour round the mountain as views open out to the south and west. Sticking to the main track you pass a stand of towering poplars next to the farm of **El Realenguillo**. Here, angling right, the track reaches a fork.

Here bear left, still following Camino de Santiago waymarking. The track runs on, fairly level, between groves of olives before dividing just before it reaches the farm buildings of **El Cortijo de Alhaja**. Bearing left past the farm the track runs parallel to a row of almond trees which retain the bank to your left. Olive groves give way to open fields as the track runs gently downhill in a westerly direction. Crossing a rise you reach a junction (**1hr 25min**).

Here turn right, immediately passing another sign for 'Santiago' and continue up a broad track towards La Sierra de Chimenea. You're now following the old drovers' path of El Cordel de Antequera. Follow the track steeply up across open farmland, ignoring a track which cuts in right towards a green and white tractor shed. Crossing a streambed the track narrows, now somewhat overgrown although its course is clear enough. It improves as it runs up to a junction with a broad track. Here turn right and follow a sign 'Camino Escaleruela, SLA22'.

At a point where the track becomes concreted you'll see a sign pointing right for 'La Escaleruela'. Ignoring this sign continue up the broad track which loops left then right before resuming its course towards the southern face of La Sierra de Chimenea. The track swings slightly left then angles right past a pylon with a concrete base to reach a junction with another broad track (**2hr 50min**).

Here turn left and begin to descend, immediately passing gates leading to a **farm** which clings to the southern slope of La Sierra de Chimenea. Bearing left the track passes the buildings of **Cortijo la Fuenfría**. Just past the farm you pass the six stone troughs of the eponymous Fuenfría. ▶ The track crosses a rise. The mountains behind Valle de Abdalajís come into sight along with the distant Guadalhorce reservoir. The track loops more

Fuenfría literally means 'cold spring' although its plastic exit pipe makes it more of a hot spring when the sun is shining.

Cloud descending over the mountains to the east of Valle de Abdalajís

If you wish to replenish your water supply there's a spring, La Fuente de la Higuera, just beyond the barrier on the other side of the road.

steeply downwards before it runs up to a 'Stop' sign where it meets the MA-437. Here turn right. ◄

Follow the road past a large concrete **water tank** just to the left of the road. Descending you pass a 'No Overtaking' sign then a house with a row of cypress trees where the road arcs hard right. Here, reaching a 'Stop' sign and another for 'Valle de Abdelajis/Las Cuerdas/El Castillo/El Bermejal', turn left off the road (**4hr 20min**).

You pass a **white hut** then 90m later reach a fork. Here bear right, sticking to the main track. After climbing slightly the track loops down past a rocky outcrop, passes above a farm building then runs on past the gates of Finca las Cuerdas then a plastic-lined reservoir. ◄

Views open out towards the flatter countryside to the north and northwest.

Passing left of a modern house, **Villa de Paqui**, the track loops round another rocky outcrop then bears right before reaching a junction next to a breeze-block shed. Here keep right and continue past the buildings of **Cortijo del Castillo** beyond which you reach a three-way divide in the track. Ignoring a marker post pointing straight ahead, cut left down a steep track. At the next fork, marked 'Coto Privado de Caza', keep left.

The track descends more steeply before crossing the streambed of Arroyo del Búho then climbs steeply up to reach a junction. Angling hard right you pass beneath **Cortijo de la Fuente de la Zarza**. The track levels then begins to descend before running up to another junction (**5hr 15min**).

Head straight on towards Valle de Abdalajís across more open terrain between groves of almonds. After passing beneath three runs of power lines the track bears hard right, once more left, then crosses the Arroyo de las Piedras. Angling slightly right then passing a fading map of the GR7 the track runs up to reach the first houses in the village.

Head straight on beneath a high wall built of rocks then follow the road round to the right to reach a junction with the **A-343**. Cross the A-343, passing just right of a statue of Madre Petra, and continue along Calle Madre Petra. Reaching Plaza Virgen de los Dolores head on past a 'No Entry' sign along Calle Real. Passing a bank you reach the village's main square and its *mercado municipal* (municipal market) next to a fountain with a ceramic map (**6hr**).

VALLE DE ABDALAJÍS (POPULATION 2955, ALTITUDE 339M)

The valley that leads north past Valle de Abdalajís has long served as a thoroughfare to the rich farmlands of the *vega* or plain of Antequera. Palaeolithic axe and arrow heads and Iberian votive offerings have been found close to the present village while during the Roman period Seneca referred to a settlement here called Nescania. The pedestal of a statue of Trajan can still be seen in the Plaza de San Lorenzo. Destroyed by the Vandals in the 4th century, the Moors under Abid Al-Aziz founded a new settlement in the 8th century from which the present village takes its name.

Statue of Ana Josefa Pérez aka Madre Petra

The village was the birthplace in 1845 of Ana Josefa Pérez, better known as Madre Petra, who was a kind of local Mother Teresa. She dedicated her life to the old and homeless, founding no less than ten hospices in the region. She died in 1906 and was beatified by Pope John Paul II in 1994. In the village a convent and street both bear her name.

The town, in best Andaluz style, celebrates Carnival and Holy Week to the full while its annual *feria* (fair) coincides with the Feast Day of its patron saint, San Lorenzo, in early August. On 24 June, La Noche de San Juan, villagers takes part in an extended water fight while an annual pilgrimage up to the chapel of Cristo de la Sierra begins with a short mass which is followed by music, merriment and copious quantities of food and wine.In spite of being well off the tourist trail – one of the place's principal charms – the village has seen an influx of foreigners over the past few years thanks to the arrival of the paragliding community along with walkers and climbers, while the recent opening of El Caminito del Rey (see Day 10) has brought welcome custom to the village's hotels and bars.

Two elegant buildings dating back to the 16th century are worth a look: the Palacio del Conde de los Corbos and the Antigua Posada.

Recommended accommodation
Hostal Vista a la Sierra €€
Bookings via **www.booking.com**
Friendly B&B with great views from its valley-facing rooms.

Recommended accommodation close to the village
Hotel Refugio del Alamut €–€€
www.refugioalamut.com
An attractive rural hotel on the west side of the valley just 1 kilometre north of the village.

Contacts
Ayuntamiento: **www.valledeabdalajis.es**
Taxi: Paco 679 423 635

DAY 10
Valle de Abdalajís to Carratraca via El Chorro

Start	In front of the municipal market, Valle de Abdalajís
Distance	25.8km
Ascent/Descent	1100m/910m
Grade	Difficult
Time	7hr 30min
Map	IGN 1:50000 Ardales 1038
Refreshments	Bars and restaurants in El Chorro

This unforgettable day of walking takes in some of the most spectacular scenery encountered on the Coast to Coast Walk. The route begins with a steady climb along the flank of the Sierra de Abdalajís to La Fuente de la Viuda then on past the sheer cliff face of the Sierra de Huma.

As you approach El Chorro, now descending, sheer rock faces rise higher and higher to the north where you'll see large numbers of griffon vultures (*Gyps fulvus*) riding the thermals high above the gorge.

From the railside settlement of El Chorro you're faced with a steep climb up to the reservoir above the village from where water is fed down to the village's hydro-electric plant. Cutting past the archaeological site of Bobastro – programme in at least half an hour for this fascinating visit – you soon leave the tarmac road behind as you continue towards Carratraca, by way of farm tracks. Later you pick up a narrow path which winds slowly westwards before looping down to the village.

The stage can be split into two easier days by breaking the journey at El Chorro. Due to the popularity of the Caminito del Rey you'll need to book a room well in advance. If you plan to walk the Caminito be sure to book a place several weeks in advance.

The stage begins in the small square in front of the *mercado municipal* (municipal market) in Valle de Abdalajís.

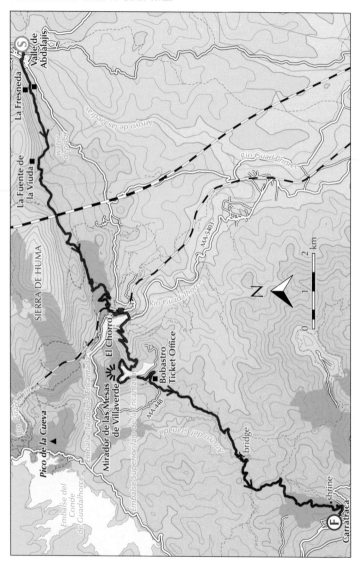

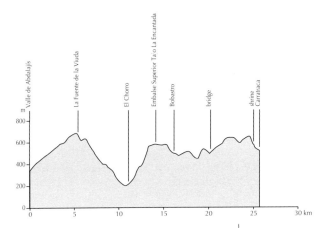

With your back to the market turn right then take the first right up Calle Alameda then pass just left of the *ayuntamiento* (town hall). At the top of the street climb a flight of steps then bear left along Calle Siles then angle hard right past a 9T weight limit sign. Reaching a sign pointing back the way you came for 'Club de Vuelo' bear hard left along Calle Alta. Leaving the last of the village's houses behind, follow a concrete track parallel to the southern face of the Sierra de Abdalajís.

Soon the concrete ends. Continue along a broad, dirt track which runs gently upwards. ▸ The track runs past the first buildings of the hamlet of **La Fresneda** (**30min**) then looping left reaches a junction and a 'Stop' sign. Turn right here and head on parallel to the steep cliffs of the Sierra de Abdalajís. The tarmac road, climbing, runs past a large **water deposit** before reaching another junction.

Here follow the tarmac road round to the right then climb steeply past an overhanging rock face. Tarmac gives way to concrete as views open out to the southwest. The track reaches a fork and a sign for 'Paraje Natural' and another pointing back the way you've just come for 'Valle de Abdalajís'.

To your left a viaduct on the Madrid–Málaga high-speed railway line comes into view.

Taking the left fork head down past a white house beyond which you reach another junction. Here bear hard right along a broad dirt track, immediately passing a concrete junction box. After running fairly level the track loops right, climbs steeply, then runs past an isolated farm. Beyond the farm you reach **La Fuente de la Viuda** spring with a run of six drinking troughs and ancient wash stones (**1hr 30min**). ◄

This is a beautiful spot to rest and replenish your water.

Beyond the spring the track drops down to reach a junction. Here bear right following GR249 waymarking and a sign 'El Chorro 5.8km'. ◄ Running past ruins to either side the track passes the buildings of another farm. Passing through a green metal-gated shed continue along the track as it bears left and after 150m reaches a junction. Here turn right at a sign 'El Chorro 1hr'.

From this point you'll be following the GR249 all the way to Carratraca.

The track, rougher underfoot, climbs gently for 300m then, reaching a sign prohibiting access to motorised vehicles, angles left and descends, parallel to the southern flank of the Sierra de Huma, shortly passing just to

Limestone strata close to La Fuente de la Viuda

the right of a pylon. Reaching another junction ignore a track angling up right but rather continue descending on your same course to reach another junction next to twin signboards about local walks. Bear right here and continue down the track which descends through a swathe of pine forest. ▸

The track arcs lazily left then right then runs closer to the cliff face. Looping on down it crosses a streambed before reaching another junction. Here bear hard right towards the cliff face, shortly crossing the streambed once again at a point where it's shored up with netted boulders.

The track eventually drops down past a metal barrier then a small ruin where it arcs right before running on past a eucalyptus grove. Shortly a track merges with yours by a sign 'Sendero Haza del Río'. Bearing left you reach the first houses of **El Chorro**.

On the far side of the valley you'll spot the curtain dam of the reservoir high above El Chorro and will almost certainly see griffon vultures riding the thermals high above you.

EL CAMINITO DEL REY, EL CHORRO

When the dam and reservoir of El Chorro were created in the 1920s a hanging walkway was constructed along the edge of the gorge to give access to the hydro-electric installations. It came to be known as El Caminito del Rey following a visit by King Alfonso XIII in 1921. The path, which was closed for many years due to its perilous condition, was recently renovated and has become one of Málaga province's top tourist attractions.

If you plan to walk the Caminito you should book your ticket several weeks in advance via the website. You'll see the path clinging improbably to the sheer face of the gorge from El Mirador de las Mesas de Villaverde which you pass later in this stage.

www.caminitodelrey.info

Due to the growing popularity of El Caminito, there is a huge amount of accommodation on offer for all budgets in and around El Chorro. The author's personal favourite is Complejo Turistico La Garganta (www.lagarganta.com), which is close to the train station and just a short walk from the southern entrance of El Caminito.

At the next junction bear right then reaching a grey railing cut left and head on into the village. Just before you reach a generating station cut right at a bench, drop

El Chorro seen from the path leading up to El Embalse Superior Tajo de la Encantada

down a flight of steps, then turn right and go along the **MA-5403** to reach a drinking fountain (**3hr 10min**).

Follow the road as it loops left past Bar El Caminito then, angling right, crosses the dam spanning the southern end of the reservoir of El Chorro. Reaching the west side of the dam bear right along the MA-5403 following a sign 'Ruinas de Bobastro'. After 400m, reaching the km11 post and a signboard marking the beginning of the Ardales–El Chorro leg of the GR249, cut left up a dirt track. The track soon bears right. Reaching a GR249 marker post turn left up a narrow footpath. ◄

Steel yourself for a long, steep ascent.

Climbing steeply the sandy path passes to the left of a sheer rock face. ◄ Reaching a stand of pines the path runs up towards the curtain dam of the reservoir high above El Chorro, **El Embalse Superior Tajo de la Encantada**. Reaching a track just below the reservoir angle right up towards a tarmac road.

At this stage the path has been gouged out of solid rock: it can be slippery in wet weather.

Just before you reach the road and a gate angle slightly right, continue parallel to the road for 25m then bear right again along a tarmac road which adopts a course more or less parallel to the side of the reservoir.

After 150m, just before you pass beneath overhead power lines, to your left you'll see a chain linking a gap in two metal crash barriers. Cut left through the gap then follow a track that runs on round the reservoir.

After passing a viewing point, **Mirador de las Mesas de Villaverde**, from where the Caminito del Rey is visible, the track passes a metal barrier then meets the **MA-448 (5hr 25min)**. Turn right down the tarmac road. ▶ After describing a lazy loop the road passes the **ticket hut** for the ruins of the citadel fortress of Bobastro.

It's possible to walk along a narrow path just to the right of its crash barrier.

> **Bobastro** was the mountain refuge and power base of the rebel *muladí* (a convert to Islam during the Moorish occupation of Spain) leader Omar Ben Hafsun who, at the end of the 9th century, led a rebellion against the great Emirate of Córdoba. Towards the end of his life, still undefeated, he converted to Christianity: the remains of the church that he built at Bobastro are the only *Mozarabic* (relating to Christians who lived in Moorish Spain) place of worship to have survived from the Moorish period. He died in 917 leaving his sons in charge of the uprising. Bobastro eventually fell to the forces of the Emirate in 928.
>
> The archaeological site should not be missed. Opening times: Tues–Sun 10am–3pm

Continuing on down the MA-448 for 250m you reach a sign 'Ubicación Parkings'. Here cut left away from the tarmac along a broad dirt track. You soon pass by Casa Bolero then the entrance gates to Villa Cabrera. At the end of its fenced land you reach a fork where you should keep right, shortly passing another small house with a pool as you head along the top of a ridge.

Reaching another fork bear right: you immediately pass by the gates of Casa de la Zamarrilla. At the next fork keep left. Passing another house with a high chimney the track descends, passes left of a water deposit, then runs on between almond groves. Bearing right past the gates of Rancho del Goina it runs past a huge pylon. At the next

113

fork, some 75m past the pylon, keep right, sticking to the main track, high above the streambed of the **Arroyo del Granado** which is now down to your right.

The track runs up to another more major junction (**6hr 5min**). Take the track to the right following GR249 waymarking. Soon you pass Finca José El Pavito as the track runs on through almond groves interspersed with evergreen oaks. Looping left it climbs as it passes by a track cutting down to Casa Chaparral de Colilla. Here it loops hard to the right, still climbing steeply. Crossing a concrete storm drain you reach a junction.

Branch right following GR249 waymarking. Descending steeply past a small white hut to the valley floor you cross a **bridge** signed '*Inundable*' (subject to flooding). Beyond the bridge the track loops upwards as it enters a stand of pine trees. Cypress trees line its left side. Sections of the track are surfaced with damaged tarmac as it runs on up to reach a junction. ◄ Take the left fork following the GR249 sign 'Carratraca 4.4km' along a dirt track which continues to ascend. Looking back east you can now see a large swathe of the terrain that you covered earlier in the walk.

At this point the GR7 and GR249 diverge.

Path descending through the pine forest towards Carratraca

Angling left then right the track runs along a ridge-top as a wind generator comes into view to your right. Passing through a gap in a fence it levels for a short distance then begins to descend. A fence soon runs to your right. Following the fence as it angles hard right the track runs steeply upwards. Cutting right, away from the track, through a gap in the fence – it's waymarked – continue along a narrow, sandy footpath which immediately runs past a line of fig trees. A fence now runs to your left.

Reaching a gap in the fence, at a post marked with red and white paint flashes, cut left and follow the path down through the pines which eventually angles hard left then passes a small **shrine** dedicated to the Virgen de la Salud. The path widens as the first houses of **Carratraca** come into view.

Looping sharply left the path again arcs right then runs up to a junction. Here branch left down a narrower path which loops steeply down to reach a junction next to a GR249 signboard at the outskirts of the village. Turning right you soon pass the village's flamboyant ayuntamiento. Head along a one-way street past Fonda Pepa then angle left to reach the main square of the village, La Plaza de la Constitución (**7hr 30min**).

CARRATRACA (POPULATION 870, ALTITUDE 538M)

Lying at the base of the Sierra de Alcaparaín and to one side of the fertile Guadalhorce valley which cuts northwest through the mountains from Málaga, Carratraca – the name comes from the Arabic Karr Al-Krak or 'cleansing place of wounds' – was the gateway between the coast and the rich agricultural lands stretching north towards Campillos and Antequera. Cave paintings from the Palaeolithic era in the nearby Doña Trinidad cave depicting goats, horses and deer suggest that the area was a rich hunting ground for early Iberian Man.

The sulphurous springs which well up within the present village have attracted settlement since the times of the Romans who extolled the curative properties of its waters. There was a small settlement here during the Moorish period but it was from the mid-19th through to the early 20th century that the town was to live its golden age at a time when taking the waters became fashionable throughout Spain.

Carratraca's flamboyant tourist office

The grandeur of the original spa buildings belies the sleepy nature of the present settlement while the bullring and adjacent bar – you pass them at the end of Day 10 – speak of an age when the town attracted the well-heeled folk from Málaga and further afield. It was then that Doña Trinidad Grund built the flamboyant home which would later become the town hall. Illustrious visitors from that period included Lord Byron, the Empress Marie Eugenie and the poet Rainer Maria Rilke.

The baths are still open from 15 June to 15 October every year and attract a trickle of visitors. But a recent spa hotel project within some of the original buildings closed just a couple of years after its ostentatious opening.

The village's most interesting festivity takes place on the first weekend in September, El Embrujo de la Luna Mora: literally The Spell of the Moorish Moon. Stalls are set up, exotic outfits donned and *Moro* (Moorish) ceases to have any pejorative undertones. Another well-known festivity is the Easter passion play which is performed in the bullring on Good Friday and Easter Sunday.

Recommended accommodation
Fonda Casa Pepa €
952 458 049 or 686 401 610
A quirkily old-fashioned inn and an unforgettable highlight of a visit to Carratraca.

Recommended accommodation close to the village
Apartamentos Ardales €€
www.apartamentosardales.es
Swish apartments at 5km, in the centre of Ardales, 5km northwest of Carratraca.

Hotel Cortijo San Antonio €€
www.hotelcortijosanantonio.com
Roadside inn with characterful rooms and good food 6km south of Carratraca.

Contacts
Ayuntamiento: **www.carratraca.es**
Taxi: Paqui 680 539 393

DAY 11
Carratraca to El Burgo

Start	La Plaza de la Constitución, Carratraca
Distance	22.8km
Ascent/Descent	785m/750m
Grade	Medium/Difficult
Time	6hr 45min
Map	IGN 1:50000 Ardales 1038, Alora 1052, Ronda 1051
Refreshments	None en route

The captivating eleventh stage of the Coast to Coast Walk leads you through pine forest and wild mountain terrain from where there are soaring views to all points of the compass.

The day begins with a long uphill pull as you leave Carratraca and follow broad forestry tracks up to Puerto Martínez, the highest point of the stage. From the top of the pass you have a short section of tarmac to negotiate but you'll encounter few cars on this remote, country road. Cutting away from the asphalt you pick up the old drovers' path that led from Málaga to Ronda.

Be ready for a couple of more tricky sections as you climb to the ridgetop close to the ruined farms of Cortijos del Pilar. While this part of the walk is marked by cairns a handheld GPS device would make navigation much easier.

The stage begins in the main square of Carratraca, La Plaza de la Constitución. With your back to the *correos* (post office) exit the square at its bottom, left-hand corner down Calle Málaga. Reaching a roundabout at the bottom of the street angle right across the road then passing right of a tiled fountain drop down a steep street. Where the road splits four ways just beyond house no. 16 take the second street from the left, passing left of a breeze-block wall, and continue steeply on down. After passing right of a house with potted geraniums decorating its facade you descend to reach the **A-357**. Here bear right

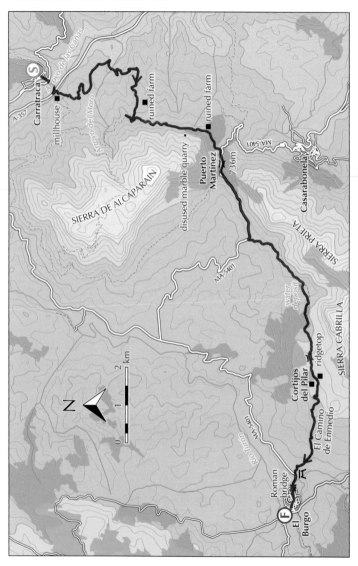

then cut left through a tunnel beneath the road. Angling left then once more right the track descends and crosses the oleander-lined course of the **Arroyo de las Cañas**.

At 75m beyond the stream you pass between the buildings of a **millhouse**. Climb steeply on up, ignoring a concreted track that cuts steeply up to the right. The track bears left by a stand of eucalyptus, crosses a streambed, then arcing once more right continues its steep ascent passing a citrus grove to your right. Following the track to the right past a small white house you reach a junction with another track.

Here turn left. The track soon adopts a course parallel to the A-357 as it runs on between olive and almond groves, passing goat sheds then a villa with Grecian urns atop the columns of its gates. Here the track arcs right then passes above a farmhouse flanked by steep terraces. Bearing back to the left the track runs along a high ridge where it becomes concreted and begins to gradually descend, passing several smallholdings. ▶ Eventually the track runs steeply down to a junction by a pylon (**1hr**).

Here turn right and go along a dirt track which drops down towards the valley floor. Looping right it passes the entrance gate of Las Minas before crossing the streambed of the **Arroyo del Moro** by a stand of eucalyptus.

Water deposits, irrigated vegetable plots and citrus groves bear witness to the abundance of water in this part of the sierra.

119

The hillsides surrounding Carratraca are peppered with **mine shafts**, whence the name of the farm of Las Minas. Between the 1850s and the 1960s nickel was worked while chromium and other metal sulphides were also extracted. During the 1960s a number of companies and individuals came to the area to prospect for diamonds. Only small, impure carbonaceous stones were found and nearly all of the prospectors left empty-handed.

Beyond the stream the track climbs through the pines with the stream over to your right. Reaching a junction where one track loops hard right, carry straight on up the left bank of the stream passing a sign 'Junta de Andalucía, Sierras de Aguas y Jarrales'.

After a steep climb you reach a three-way junction where two tracks come up from the left to meet the one you've been following. Take the right fork and continue climbing. The track soon cuts across an open swathe of ground towards the eastern face of La Sierra de Alcaparaín. Swinging sharply right then once more left it runs on towards the flank of the sierra. At this stage, to

The track leading up towards La Sierra de Alcaparaín

The old marble quarry close to Puerto Martínez

your left, you'll spot a **ruined farm**. Soon the track angles right then runs up to a broader track where there is a tiled map marked 'Puerto Martínez 4.3km' (**2hr 10m**)

Here turn left and follow a broad track on round the mountainside, still climbing gradually upwards. Huge views open out to the east towards the ranges traversed earlier on the Coast to Coast Walk. The track passes a **disused marble quarry** to the right of the track. ▶

Contouring round the hillside the track runs through a stand of oaks then passes above a **ruined farm**. It then adopts a gentle downhill course before, bearing right, it meets the **MA-5401**. Angle right across the road and follow an indistinct track down to reach a more clearly defined track. Here bear right and climb, parallel to the road, following the old *cañada* (drovers' path). Angling up to the road just beyond the km16 post you pass a sign marking **Puerto Martínez**, even though you're not quite at the top of the rise. Continue up the MA-5401 for 300m to reach the highest point of the day at 736m (**3hr 45min**).

From the top of the pass continue down the M-5401. The road runs past Cortijo del Perdigón, down to its right,

Megaliths hewn from the mountainside remain as they were left when the quarry was abandoned.

then angling right reaches a ceramic sign to the left of the road, just before the km14 marker post, for 'Cañada Real de Ronda, Camino de Ronda a Málaga'. Here turn left then after 25m bear left again along a stony track which runs gently upwards, parallel to the northwestern flank of **Sierra Prieta**. Passing high above a ruined farm the track begins to descend, now more overgrown. Crossing a streambed the track narrows then passes just left of another ruined farm and enters a stand of pines.

Sticking to the lower edge of the pines you pass through a stand of poplars where the path passes through a wire-and-post gate (**4hr 30min**) then runs parallel to the left bank of a stream. Some 75m beyond the gate angle right across the streambed then bear left up an indistinct path which climbs into the pine trees. Look for cairns and don't expect to see a clear path.

Breaking out into more open ground the path loops on up, now on a course towards the southwestern end of the **Sierra Cabrilla**. At a larger cairn the path bears right, crosses a swathe of scree, then reaches a broad track where, to your right, you'll see an old **water deposit**. Bear right along the track, ignoring a less distinct track which runs just beneath it. A few metres beyond a concrete bridge with a quintuple run of drainage channels you reach a rocky outcrop to your left.

Here cut left away from the track. Passing a black and white 'Coto' sign climb up into the pines following an indistinct path which is marked by cairns. Soon the path crosses a dry streambed. As you climb across more open terrain up ahead you'll see a rocky outcrop with a dead tree just left of its highest point. You'll be crossing the ridge about 100m left of the outcrop's southern/left-hand edge. Still climbing you reach the edge of a field which will be ploughed or covered by a crop, depending on the season. Bear right along the bottom edge of the field for some 20m then turn left then climb up through the field to the **ridgetop** which you should cross just left of a cairn and a black and white 'Coto' sign (**5hr 45min**).

Maintaining your course beyond the ridgetop drop down to a track which passes to the right of another rocky outcrop with a ruin to its left. Becoming more clearly defined it crosses two streambeds. Angling right then left the track runs past an old *alberca* (water deposit) then passes above another ruined farm, one of the **Cortijos del Pilar**. Soon you reach a four-way junction where tracks cut right and left to the two ruins.

Head straight on: you're now following the old cart track known locally as **El Camino de Enmedio**. ▸ Fields give way to groves of olive and almonds as you descend, with a fence running to your right. The track loops steeply down across more open terrain before it levels, passes the **picnic area** of Los Guerreros, then meets the MA-5401.

Turning left you cross the old **Roman bridge**. Take the next turning left and climb a concrete road, with a stone wall running just to its left, into the village. At the next fork bear left past a spring along Calle Málaga to a small square with a circular seating area at its midst. Here bear right and drop down Calle Mesones. Passing Hotel La Casa Grande del Burgo you reach La Plaza de Abajo (**6hr 45min**).

El Burgo comes into view to the west.

Heading down towards El Burgo along the flank of the Sierra Cabrilla

EL BURGO (POPULATION 2091, ALTITUDE 563M)

El Burgo fans out around a limestone outcrop close to the banks of the Turón river. A defensive tower existed here at the time of the Carthaginians while during the Roman period it became an important trading post on the road that led from Acinipo, the main Roman settlement close to Ronda, through the mountains to Málaga.

The Moors knew the settlement as El Borch from which the village takes its name. During the Islamic period the village came under the sway of the rebel leader Omar Ben Hafsun (see Bobastro section, Day 10). It took none other than Abdarrahman III, the great Emir then Caliph of Córdoba who consolidated the power of the Umayyad dynasty in Al Andalus, to defeat the descendants of the rebel chief and in 921 El Borch was recaptured by the Caliph's army.

Later, when the Caliphate splintered into several 'Taifa' kingdoms, the village came under the sway of Ronda then later the Sultanate of Granada. It was at this time that El Borch became known as a source of flint for the manufacture of spears and arrows, a tradition that was to continue after the Reconquest.

The village remained an isolated, mountain enclave for several centuries with an economy based on the cultivation of cereals, grapes, olives and almonds. This was to change in the 20th century when the arrival of motorised transport linked the town with Ronda and Málaga, while the creation of the Parque Natural de la Sierra de las Nieves has brought rural tourism to the area. There are a number of marked walking routes leading out from the village including the GR7 and GR249 footpaths with which Day 12 of the Coast to Coast Walk coincides.

The village's annual *feria* (fair) is held at the end of August while the unique Fiesta de La Sopa de los Siete Ramales takes place every year on 28 February in honour of the village's best known culinary invention, a soup based on seven ingredients: tomato, red pepper, onion, garlic, bread, mint and wild asparagus which is gathered on the mountainside during winter and spring.

Recommended accommodation
Hotel La Casa Grande del Burgo €€
www.hotel-lacasagrande.com
A comfortable village-centre hotel a few metres from the end point of the Day 11.

Hostal Sierra de las Nieves €
952 160 117
Simple hostel with a restaurant.

Contacts
Ayuntamiento: **www.elburgo.es**
Taxi: nearest taxi in Yunquera, Borja 646 009 590

DAY 12
El Burgo to Ronda

Start	La Plaza de Abajo, El Burgo
Distance	26.3km
Ascent/Descent	755m/590m
Grade	Difficult
Time	7hr 15min
Map	IGN 1:50000 Ronda 1051
Refreshments	None en route

The longish twelfth day of the Coast to Coast Walk leads through a wild swathe of the Sierra de las Nieves Natural Park to the hilltop town of Ronda, the largest town that you encounter between the two seas. Much of the stage is by way of forestry and farm tracks yet until you get within a couple of kilometres of Ronda you'll encounter few walkers or vehicles.

The early section of the stage entails a long, steady climb parallel to the beautiful valley of the Río Turón. You then follow a narrow footpath which loops down then crosses the Turón's upper reaches before leading you up to the remote farmstead of Cortijo de Lifa. A final steep climb leads to the highest point of the stage, the Puerto de Lifa. At 1169m it's nearly twice the altitude of your point of departure.

From here the track drops down to the broad plain on Ronda's eastern flank which marks the boundary between the Sierra de las Nieves and the Sierra de Grazalema. Heading on through Ronda's northeastern suburb of San Rafael you arrive at the nerve centre of the town, the small square next to the town's extraordinary gorge and its Puente Nuevo.

The stage begins in the lower square of El Burgo, La Plaza de Abajo, just below Hotel Casa Grande del Burgo. Exit the square at its bottom right-hand corner past the Cajamar bank along Calle Ronda. The street angles left as it becomes Calle Las Erillas then arrives at a roundabout. Turning left past an ironmongers you come to a junction with the **A-366**. Turn left and follow a signpost for

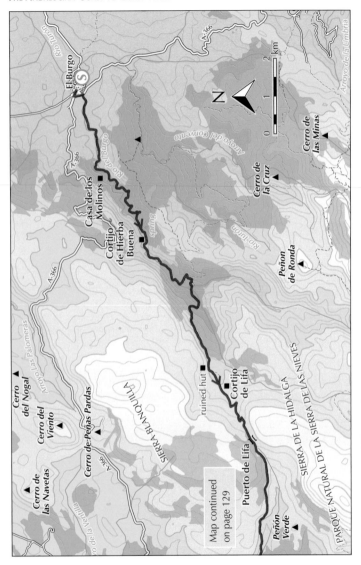

Map continued
on page 129

126

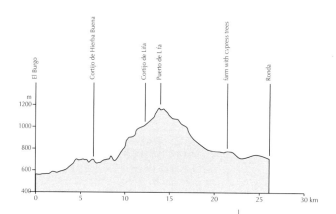

'Málaga'. After 150m you cross the Río Turón. Just beyond the river, at a sign 'Ronda GR243/GR249', turn right and go along a broad track which hugs the river's left bank. Soon you reach a fork with the left branch signed 'Puerto

Dam across the Río Turón

If walking the route in warm weather it's possible to take a dip by cutting right at a sign 'Cuenca Alta Río Turón' where a path leads down to a point where the river has been shored up.

de la Mujer/La Fuensanta'. Ignore this and carry straight on along the main track following GR249 waymarking.

The track runs on between groves of olives and almonds past a number of smallholdings: as it narrows the terrain becomes more abrupt as olive groves give way to pine forest. The track loops hard left then climbs on and passes a ruined cottage, **Casa de los Molinos**, next to twin posts set in pyramidal bases (**50min**). ◄

The track descends slightly as it heads towards the Cortijo de Hierba Buena. At a point where it becomes concreted you pass a **spring** just left of the track before passing above **Cortijo de Hierba Buena**. Some 400m past the farm the track adopts a downhill course then levels as it runs closer to the river. Climbing once again you pass through an area of denser pine plantation. ◄ Eventually, just as the track passes beneath electricity lines, you reach a marker post next to an ancient oak tree indicating 'GR243/GR249 Ronda/Lifa 15,5kms' (**2hr 15min**).

As the pines thin out the higher peaks of La Sierra de las Nieves come into view to the south.

Here cut right down a narrow path. Descending for 40m the path angles hard left then drops steeply down through the pines, marked by GR posts, to reach the Río Turón which you cross by another marker post. Beyond the stream the path loops left, running parallel to the stream's right bank for 150m before bearing right then climbing steeply. GR waymarking and cairns guide you upwards. Angling right across a more open swathe of hillside the path swings once more left as it climbs through denser undergrowth then passes through a wire-and-post gate (**2hr 35min**).

The path, now more overgrown, runs towards a steep rock face where it arcs right, climbs steeply then bears once more left before passing 10m right of a pylon marked with GR flashes. Here it adopts a course more or less parallel to the overhead electricity lines. ◄ Soon the path widens then crosses two scree slopes. The track levels as it runs past a **ruined hut** beyond which it arcs left and runs up to a green metal gate leading into the fenced enclosure of **Cortijo de Lifa**. Immediately beyond the gate turn right, follow the fence to its far end, then exit the enclosure through an identical gate.

Views open out across La Sierra de las Nieves, and up ahead you'll spot a ruined tower atop a pinnacle of rock which you'll later pass to its right.

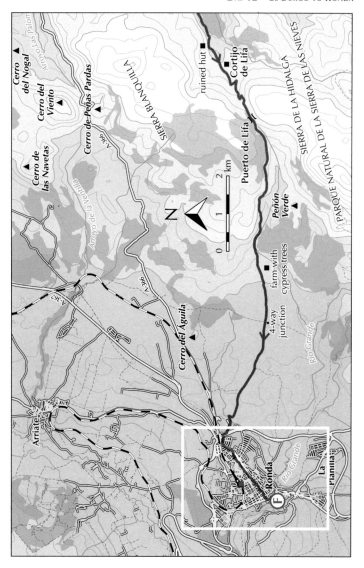

Summer landscape between La Sierra de las Nieves and Ronda

Beyond the gate the path merges with a track leading to the farmhouse. Here bear right. After passing through a third metal gate the track runs past Lifa's sheep and goat sheds. Follow the looping track to the top of the rise: you can cut corners. The track levels as it runs across an open swathe of land before climbing once more, passing through a gate then immediately crossing a cattle grid. A few metres beyond the grid you reach the highest point of the stage, the **Puerto de Lifa**, marked by a GR 243/249 signpost indicating 'Ronda 9.3 kms' (**4hr 5min**).

Ronda comes into view as the track descends then passes through a second set of gates where it crosses a second cattle grid. Eventually the track levels as it runs past a small **farm** surrounded by a dense row of cypress trees. Continue straight on, following a line of electricity pylons. At a **four-way junction** by another farm maintain your course, still following GR249 waymarking.

The track crosses a rise then descends as its dirt surface turns to tarmac (**5hr 55min**). Eventually it loops right, crosses a bridge, then bearing back left runs along the boundary fence of the grounds where Ronda's annual *feria* (fair) is held. Bearing right past a warehouse you reach a footbridge. Cut left across the bridge then

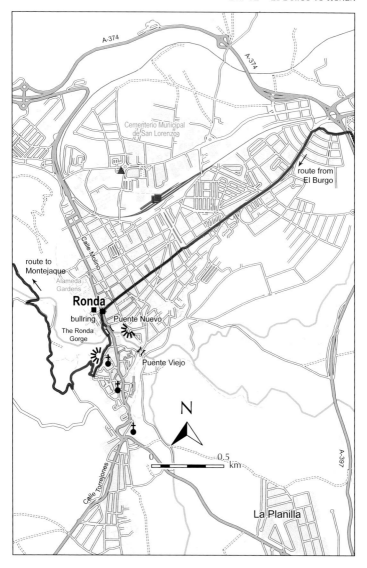

continue past four blocks of flats to reach a junction with the Avenida de Málaga.

Turning left you shortly pass a petrol station then the Guardía Civil headquarters then reach a junction by Bar Los Cazadores where, to your right, you'll see an underground car park. Here continue straight on down a pedestrianised street, Calle Vicente Espinel. At the far end of the street turn left. After 75m you reach the square in front of Ronda's most famous landmark, the Puente Nuevo, spanning the spectacular Río Guadalevín gorge (**7hr 15min**).

RONDA (POPULATION 35,440, ALTITUDE 728M)

Ronda's famous gorge and the Puente Nuevo

Dubbed Ciudad Soñada by its local council, Ronda really can lay claim to being a Town of Dreams with a physical setting that is without rival in southern Spain.

The town occupies a high plateau through which, over the millennia, the Río Guadalevín has cut a deep gorge. Known simply as El Tajo by locals, this plunging abyss is spanned by an extraordinary bridge, the Puente Nuevo, an architectural arabesque that can't fail to excite the most travel-weary eyes.

A favoured destination on the Grand Tour the town attracted poets, actors, painters and aesthetes: the likes of Rilke, David Roberts, Orson Welles, Hemingway and Bomberg were all bewitched by the beauty of the place while James Joyce waxed lyrical about the gorge on the final page of Ulysses.

The town's high plateau has seen human presence since Neolithic times and in all likelihood long before that: the troglodytes who painted symbols and animals in the Cueva de la Pileta during the Palaeolithic period would almost certainly have looked out from this extraordinary natural vantage point. The Romans built an important urbis which they knew as Arunda and from which the town takes its name. The Visigoths would oust them from Spain in the 5th century and continued to occupy Ronda, building one of Spain's earliest Christian churches on a hillside just south of the town.During the Moorish period the town began to take on its present-day appearance. A sizeable slice of the old town wall bears witness to their presence as does the extraordinary subterranean passage of La Mina which gave access to the Guadalevín river, and water, in times of siege. Ronda became a key settlement on Granada's western frontier and only fell to the Christians in 1485. Much of the town east of the gorge is built on the foundations of the Moorish settlement while the minaret of the principal mosque was converted into a belfry.

The town would only see westward expansion once the Puente Nuevo was completed in 1793. That same decade saw the opening of its most famous civic building, La Plaza de Toros, where the rules of the modern bullfight were laid down and where the Romero and Ordoñez dynasties would make Ronda synonymous with the fighting of bulls or *tauromaquía*.

Recommended accommodation
Ronda has a huge choice of accommodation. Among the author's favourites are:

Hotel San Gabriel €€
www.hotelsangabriel.com
A homely, family-run hotel at the heart of the old town.

Alavera de los Baños €€
www.alaveradelosbanos.com
Next to the Arab baths in the lower part of the town with a garden and pool.

Hotel San Francisco €€
www.hotelsanfrancisco-ronda.com
Spruce, well managed and keenly priced hotel in the town centre.

Hostal Restaurante La Rondeña €€
www.larondena.com
Amazing position at the edge of the gorge in a quiet pedestrianised street.

Contacts
Ayuntamiento: **www.ronda.es**
Taxi: Taxi Rank 952 874080, Esteban 606 986 666

DAY 13
Ronda to Montejaque

Start	La Plaza de España in front of the Parador, Ronda
Distance	11.7km
Ascent/Descent	410m/450m
Grade	Medium
Time	3hr 50min
Map	IGN 1:50000 Ronda 1051 & Ubrique 1050
Refreshments	None en route

The thirteenth and shortest day of the Coast to Coast Walk begins in spectacular fashion as you drop steeply down the side of the town's mesmerising *tajo* or gorge. After cutting across the broad bowl of the valley immediately south of the town along a quiet country lane you then climb steeply up to the Puerto de las Muelas. Beyond the pass you descend through pine forest before reaching the open farmland of the Guadiaro valley.

Crossing the Ronda to Algeciras railway line you then follow a steep track across the valley's western flank, through fields of wheat and olive groves, to the tiny chapel of La Escarihuela, high above Montejaque. From here an ancient cobbled track zigzags steeply down to the outskirts of the village.

During the earlier part of the stage there are fine views back to Ronda and its extraordinary Puente Nuevo.

The stage begins in front of the Ronda Parador in the square next to the bridge. With your back to the Parador turn right and cross the gorge via the Puente Nuevo. At 40m beyond the bridge turn right and go along Calle Tenorio. Continue past the Duquesa de Parcent restaurant then the Casa Don Bosco to a small square with a *mirador* (viewing point) looking out across the valley that lies to the south of the town. At the far end of the square, just beyond a seated statue, turn right. Passing a sign 'Cuidad de Ronda, Puerta de los Molinos' pick up a steep path

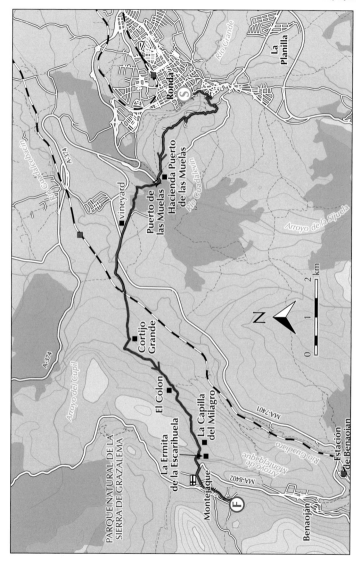

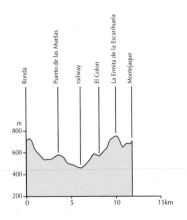

The path to the right leads down to a spectacular promontory from where you have a great view of the Ronda bridge.

which zigzags down past a ruined cottage. Descending further the path divides. Here bear left. ◄

Ronda seen from the west in winter with a snow-capped Sierra de las Nieves

PUENTE NUEVO

The Puente Nuevo, standing 98m at its highest point, was completed in 1793 and established a vital link between the old city and the more open land to the east of the gorge. A previous bridge which stood on two high pillars was destroyed when the Guadalevín was in spate after heavy winter rains. Many died and the new bridge's massive supporting pillars – they almost fill the gorge – were conceived so that such a disaster should never reoccur.

Hemingway had the bridge in mind when writing *For Whom the Bell Tolls* even though the events described in his novel took place in Aragón.

Follow the path on down through one of Ronda's Moorish gates, El Puerto del Viento, to reach a cobbled track then turn right and follow GR249 waymarking. The track winds down past a signboard depicting the birds that can be seen in the gorge. Continuing down the track towards the valley floor you reach a fork a few metres before an electricity inspection hut. Here cut left, following a sign 'Casas Rurales Ronda'. The track loops hard right, descends, then crosses the Río Guadalevín. Passing beneath the buildings of Casas Rurales Ronda the track runs on between a number of small, country dwellings. ▶

To your right Ronda's towering cliff face rises dramatically upwards.

Crossing more open countryside the track runs past Haza del Batán, its entrance gate embellished with a Crucifixion within a glass-fronted niche. Passing above a vineyard you reach a junction in front of **Hacienda Puerto de las Muelas** (**40min**). Turn right and follow the track, which now has a tarmac surface, steeply up to reach **Puerto de las Muelas**.

Some 25m beyond the pass you reach a fork. Take the left option, now following a rutted track which cuts through a stand of pines before reaching more open, scrubby ground. Bearing right you pass beneath a power line before reaching a low, white building. Here turn left down a sandy track following a GR249 sign 'Benaoján 7.8km'. Angling right the track becomes more rutted as it descends past a number of small cottages then a stand of eucalyptus before bearing hard right then running on down to merge with a broader track. Bearing right you pass a rusting grain silo. Continuing on along the edge of a **vineyard** past a line of terraced houses the track meets the **MA-7401** (**1hr 15min**).

> Until the late 1800s Ronda was a great **wine** producing area, a tradition that dated back to Roman times: coins minted at Acinipo, the nearby Roman settlement, bore the stamp of a bunch of grapes. Phyloxera killed most of the region's vines at the end of the 19th century when most farmers ceased to plant vines, but thanks to a number of pioneering vintners over the past two decades winemaking has returned to the sierra. Ronda now has some 30 small-scale *bodegas* (wineries) and several award-winning wines.

El Peñon de Mures seen on the ascent past Cortijo Grande

Here turn left then after 300m pick up a narrow path which runs just left of the MA-7401. At the point where the crash barrier ends, which has been to your right,

angle right across the road then, passing right of a line of rubbish bins, continue along a narrow country lane. You shortly pass house no. 61 where twin garden gnomes stand vigil. Passing a number of houses the track runs on southwards, crossing two tributaries of the Guadiaro before it bears hard right then crosses the **railway** via a level crossing.

Beyond the railway line the track divides. Here, ignoring GR249 waymarking pointing left, head straight on following a sign 'GR7 Montejaque 4.1kms' along a rutted dirt track that climbs steeply across open countryside towards the ruined farm of **Cortijo Grande**. Passing right of the farm the track angles left then right before continuing its steep ascent. At 250m beyond the farm the track cuts sharply left, adopting a more southerly course.

Passing the entrance gates of **El Colon** the track climbs steeply once again, now more eroded. Reaching a fork take the right-hand option, maintaining your course. After levelling, the track runs on between towering agave plants then arcs gradually right before it passes just to the right of the low, whitewashed buildings of **La Capilla del Milagro**. Maintaining your course along a narrow path across a flat meadow flanked by limestone outcrops you reach **La Ermita de la Escarihuela** (**3hr 15min**).

> **La Ermita de la Escarihuela** was built in the 18th century to commemorate the Virgen de la Escarihuela who was attributed to have saved the village from the Plague at a time when it was rife throughout the Sierra. 'Escarihuela' takes its name from the medieval Spanish word 'escarigüela' meaning a zigzagging path leading up a steep hillside.

A few metres beyond the chapel continue down a cobbled track that zigzags steeply down as Montejaque comes into view. Describing a last loop to the left the track runs past the village **cemetery** before meeting the **MA-8402**. Turn right and follow a footpath parallel to the road, shortly passing a sign 'Bienvenidos a Montejaque'.

The street takes its name from Montejaque's twin village in Germany.

Continuing along the left side of Avenida de Knittlingen past a line of recycling bins you reach a junction next to a small, corner bar. ◄ Maintaining your course you pass by the old village wash house, then Bar La Reja, then the small supermarket of La Fuente before reaching a three-way junction next to a bank. Taking the middle option you reach the main square of **Montejaque** (3hr 50min).

MONTEJAQUE (POPULATION 1009, ALTITUDE 689M)

The ceramic sign of Montejaque's 100-year-old bakery

Cradled amidst the stark limestone peaks of the Montalete, Juan Diego and Algarrobo sierras the white cluster of Montejaque's houses evokes its Berber origins. The village's name is derived from Monte Xaquez meaning 'sacred mountain' or 'hidden mountain'.

A large fortress once stood on the site of the present village which was a vital link in Nasrid Granada's western line of defence. Once a part of the jurisdiction of Ronda, the village gained autonomy following the Reconquest when along with Benaoján it was ceded to the Count of Benavente: the family's coat of arms can still be seen on a mansion house in the village square. During La Guerra de la Independencía (aka The Peninsular War) the village would gain fame when José de Águilar, a Montejaqueño, rallied a force of just 250 men to defeat a French army of 600 foot soldiers and 90 cavalry.

The limestone peaks surrounding the village are home to some of the most extensive cave systems in Andalucía and the village has a small museum dedicated to *espeleología* or caving. It includes information on the extraordinary Hundidero cavern system, which can be visited with a guide, and the Cueva de la Pileta which is 5km south of the village. The Pileta cave contains some of Spain's finest cave paintings and makes for a fascinating visit.

The tortured nature of the terrain in this part of the sierra meant that a number of Andalucía's most infamous bandoleros chose the mountains close to the village as their refuge while a number of Republicans took to the hills here during and after the Spanish Civil War.

The town's annual *feria* (fair) takes place in August while two other fiestas are held in honour of the town's patron, the Virgen de la Concepción, who is said to have saved the village from ravages of the Plague. The town is also known for its annual Juego del Cántaro when teams from the village throw an earthenware pitcher back and forth in a circle until a fumbled catch spells elimination.

Recommended accommodation
Posada del Fresno €€
www.posadadelfresno.com
Small village inn close to the main square run by a friendly Spanish couple.

Apartamentos Sierra del Hacho €
952 167 281
Spruce apartments above a tapas and breakfast bar.

Recommended accommodation close to the village
Cortijo Las Piletas €€
www.cortijolaspiletas.com
Country hotel with pool and evening meals, 5km from the village.

Contacts
Ayuntamiento: **www.montejaque.es**
Cueva de la Pileta: 952 167 343
Taxi: Alonso 607 919 352

Montejaque seen from the north

DAY 14
Montejaque to Cortes de la Frontera

Start	La Plaza de la Constitución, Montejaque
Distance	19.5km
Ascent/Descent	635m/705m
Grade	Medium/Difficult
Time	6hr
Map	IGN 1:50000 Ubrique 1050 & Cortes de la Frontera 1064
Refreshments	None en route

The fourteenth day of the Coast to Coast Walk is mostly by way of the isolated Líbar valley where you encounter just two remote farmsteads in some five hours of walking. The valley has a beauty all of its own and is flanked by some of the most remarkable karst limestone formations in Andalucía.

Once you've negotiated a steep climb out from Montejaque the track that runs along the valley floor makes for easy walking yet the mountains to either side are wild and rugged. The middle section of the stage leads you past ancient stands of deciduous and evergreen oaks: each one is a living sculpture and some would have first seen the light of day four or five hundred years ago.

To enjoy the walk to the full take plenty of water and get going early, leaving time to savour this uniquely beautiful tract of mountain terrain. And be sure to divert a few metres in from the path to take a break at the spring described midway through the walk: it's an enchantingly beautiful spot.

The stage begins on the east side of the main square in Montejaque, La Plaza de la Constitución. Cross the square, head along the left side of the church under a row of palm trees then turn right into Calle Nueva. Take the third turning to your left, opposite a building marked 'El Hogar de los Jubilados' along Calle Santa Cruz then follow the street up through the village. Leaving the last houses behind, then passing kennels in among the rocks

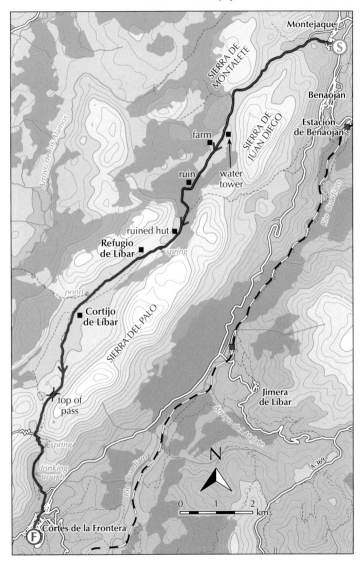

Montejaque

S

Benaojan

Estacion
de Benaojan

SIERRA DE
MONTALETE

SIERRA DE
JUAN DIEGO

farm

ruin

water
tower

Arroyo de los Álamos

ruined hut

Refugio
de Líbar

spring

pond

Cortijo
de Líbar

SIERRA DEL PALO

Rio Guadiaro

Jimera
de Líbar

Arroyo del Arrajate

top of
pass

spring

A-369

drinking
trough

N

0   1   2
km

Rio Guadiaro

Cortes de la Frontera

F

143

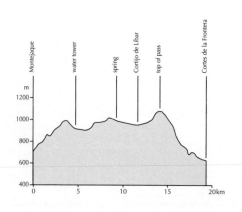

to your left you meet a track by a GR7 marker post and a signboard depicting the bird species that inhabit the valley.

Continue straight along the track, climbing between the **Sierra de Juan Diego** and the **Sierra de Montalete**. Some 550m after crossing a cattle grid you reach the top of the pass (**1hr 25min**).

Beyond the pass the track descends between two fences. Reaching the valley floor it levels as you pass a white **water tower** with solar panels. Continuing along the valley the track passes an isolated **farm** before passing through a black metal gate where there's a second signboard depicting common bird species. Running on between fences the track enters a stand of ancient gall and holm oaks before it arcs right past a **ruin**. Climbing it soon loops left then passes a sign 'Casa Rural Refugio de Líbar, 3 kms'.

The track climbs more steeply before it levels then begins to gently descend. Looping once more right it resumes its course along the valley and crosses a cattle grid before passing a **ruined hut**. Some 500m beyond the ruin the track bears right then gently left. Here, to your left, you'll see a line of saplings protected by plastic mesh. Reaching a cairn at the third meshed cage cut left, away from the track, up a narrow path for 100m to reach a **spring** where there's shade beneath a huge oak tree. ▸

Returning to the track, turn left. Continuing on your earlier course you pass two tracks which angle left towards a gate in a stone wall. Stick to the main track which arcs right, crosses a cattle grid, then runs up to a metal gate. Beyond the gate bear left following a sign 'Cortes 9km'. The track that cuts right leads to the **Refugio de Líbar**, a mountain refuge.

Head on along the valley with a fence to your left. Some 800m beyond the gate the track bears right, away from the fence. Here head straight on along a less distinct track, still just right of the fence. Passing a **pond** and a sign 'Fin de Sendero' you reach a metal gate with signs for 'Zona de Seguridad' and 'Prohibido el Paso'. The latter isn't true: you're on a public footpath which the farm owner would prefer to have to himself (**3hr 30min**).

Beyond the gate head along a faint track which runs between rows of recently planted trees. It soon angles left then cuts right, parallel to the rows of trees, then merges with a broader track which leads to the **Cortijo de Líbar**. Here, where the track angles left towards the farm, continue straight ahead along a faint vehicle track parallel to a streambed which is some 5–10m to your right. After crossing to the streambed's right bank, then back to its left bank, some 850m beyond the Cortijo de Líbar you reach a gate in the wall at the southern end of the valley.

Go through the gate and head up into the rocks, looking for cairns. Sticking to the most clearly defined path, which crosses three grassy clearings among the rocks as it ascends, you reach the top of the pass (**4hr 20min**).

Beyond the pass the path runs high above a deep, flat-bottomed valley down to your right which has two stone corrals at its northern end. The path shortly merges with a track which leads down towards the corrals. Here continue climbing for 300m then cut right at a cairn along a path which skirts round another deep hollow, also over to your right, before you pass through a

This is an exquisitely beautiful place to take a rest and replenish your water bottle.

The Cortijo de Líbar

wire-and-post gate. Beyond the gate, continuing straight ahead, you reach a track. Continue along the track to a huge cairn. Just 5m beyond the cairn bear left then after 20m cut right, away from the track, down a narrow path. Cobbled in parts, the path zigzags down between the rocks then meets the track once again (**5hr**).

Here turn right and drop down a concreted section that passes beneath a **spring** and a water trough. Follow the track as it arcs right then left then turn right down another section of path to cut off another loop. Meeting the track once again turn right and head along the valley floor. Passing through a wire-and post fence you pass a **drinking trough**. At 125m beyond the trough turn left down a narrow path. Looping right then left the path meets a track just beneath a brown metal gate.

Cross the track and continue along a path which runs above an olive grove before reaching the outskirts of **Cortes** and a group of apartment blocks. Just beyond the third block turn left down a flight of steps. Passing a children's playground take the first turning right then the

next left to reach a 'Stop' sign by a small roundabout with a statue at its midst.

Descending towards Cortes de la Frontera

Here turn right. Passing a supermarket, then a bull-ring you reach a fork in the road. Here take the left fork along Calle Real. Passing a tiled fountain then a church you reach the square of La Plaza Carlos III and its elegant *ayuntamiento* (town hall) (**6hr**).

CORTES DE LA FRONTERA (POPULATION 3700, ALTITUDE 621M)

High above the Guadiaro valley Cortes de la Frontera's streets of whitewashed buildings stand in dazzling contrast to the stark, southeastern flank of the Sierra de los Pinos. The valley has seen plenty of passing trade over the millennia: after the hunter gatherers came Phoenicians, Carthaginians, Greeks and Romans who were all to leave traces of their presence close to the present village.

Little remains of the Berber settlement of Cortex which fell to Ferdinand III in 1230 only to be reconquered by the Moors a few years later. They held on to the village for another two and a half centuries at a time when it lay on the border between Nasrid Granada and Christian Spain whence the 'de la Frontera' epithet.

The town hall in Cortes de la Frontera's Plaza de la Constitución

The municipality, which straddles both the Grazalema and the Alcornocales Natural Park, numbers among the richest in Andalucía thanks to the produce of its enormous swathe of cork oak (*Quercus Suber*) forest. The town's fortunes have long been linked with the cork harvest and the present-day village centre dates from the 1700s when systematic farming of cork oak began in the area. By the end of that century a number of fine buildings – these include the town hall, the Church of Nuestra Señora del Rosario and La Casa de Valdenebros – bore witness to the village's new-found wealth.

Like other settlements along the valley Cortes' fortunes were given a boost with the coming of the Algeciras to Ronda railway, when a station was built in the valley beneath the village. As well as opening new markets to the Cortesanos, along with the railway came tobacco and coffee which were smuggled across the border from Gibraltar then on up the line. Many of the smugglers were impoverished women who would sell their goods from the train windows: they became known as *matuteras*.

One of the municipality's least known yet most fascinating sites is the Casa de la Piedra which you pass on the next leg of the walk (see Day 15).

Recommended accommodation close to the village

Finca La Rana Verde €–€€
www.fincalaranaverde.com
Warmly welcoming riverside farmhouse accommodation in the valley beneath Cortes.

Hotel Inz-Almaraz €€
www.hotelinzalmaraz.com
Pristine small hotel in Jimera de Líbar about 7kms north of Cortes.

Contacts
Ayuntamiento: **www.cortesdelafrontera.es**
Taxi: Juan 600 219 795

DAY 15
Cortes de la Frontera to El Colmenar

Start	La Plaza de Carlos III, Cortes de la Frontera
Distance	15.8km
Ascent/Descent	515m/890m
Grade	Medium
Time	5hr
Map	IGN 1:50000 Cortes de la Frontera 1064
Refreshments	Shops and bars in Estación de Cortes

The fifteenth day of the Coast to Coast Walk runs southwards down the Guadiaro valley into the heart of the Alcornocales Natural Park. An ancient footpath first leads you down to Estación de Cortes past La Casa de la Piedra which is an essential detour.

Leaving the railside settlement you cross the Río Guadiaro then follow farm tracks south, parallel to the river, to La Casa del Conde. From here a narrow path zigzags down to the Puente de los Alemanes which spans the point where the Guadiaro valley abruptly narrows to become a steep-sided gorge, just metres wide at its narrowest point.

Beyond the bridge you're faced with a steep climb up a narrow path which levels as it runs close to the gorge's western flank. Here you're guaranteed plenty of avian action from the colony of griffon vultures (*Gyps fulvus*) that inhabits the upper reaches of the gorge's precipitous cliffs.

Following the path on past idyllic rock pools you reach El Colmenar (which is also sometimes referred to as Estación de Gaucín).

The stage begins in the main square of Cortes de la Frontera, La Plaza de Carlos III. With your back to the *ayuntamiento* (town hall) cut right, climb a flight of steps, then leave the square along Calle Nuestra Señora del Rosario. Passing Bar Los Amigos the street angles left then descends to a junction in front of a small park. Here turn right then immediately right once again past a sign for 'Ubrique'.

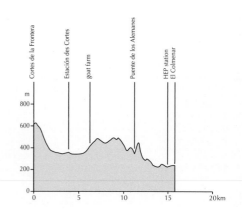

After passing a motorcycle shop angle left at a marker post down a rough track. Passing beneath two unfinished apartment blocks you reach a junction by a spring where waymarking points left, downhill. Ignore this path but rather stick to the wider track, maintaining your course.

The track gradually angles round to the east then, becoming concreted, drops down to the **A-373**. Head straight across and continue down a narrower footpath, La Vereda de Calderero, which after 30m cuts right and crosses the **Arroyo Hondo** via a small stone bridge. Continuing your descent along the old, cobbled path you reach a damaged signboard. Here cut left through a wire-and-post gate to visit **La Casa de la Piedra**.

Theories vary as to the origin of **La Casa de la Piedra** whose inner chamber and exterior decoration have been carved out of a single sandstone boulder. According to some sources it began life as a Visigothic place of worship while others claim that it was a clandestine Mozarabic chapel built by Christians for worship during the Moorish period. What's certain is that it was later used for wine making: part of the press can still be seen as well as the vats which were used to store the wine.

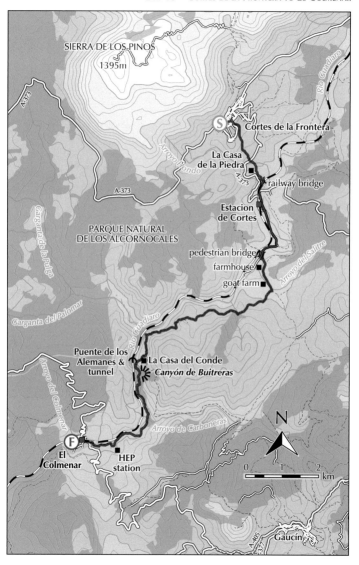

La Casa de la Piedra

Passing immediately left of a small farmhouse the path widens to become a track that leads beneath a **railway bridge**. Beyond the bridge cut right. Reaching the A-373 once again, go straight ahead. Reaching a 50kmph sign angle left at a sign 'El Gecko' then follow the road through the railside settlement of **Estación de Cortes** for approximately 1.5km. Leaving the last houses of the village behind, the river comes into sight over to your left. Passing a stand of eucalyptus and some ancient oaks you reach a **pedestrian bridge** spanning the Río Guadiaro (**1hr 20min**).

Cross the bridge then, angling left then right past a **farmhouse**, follow a rutted track up to a junction with a broader track. Here turn right and follow a sign 'Colmenar GR141 11.2km'. The track leads past a stone building marked Allá Bajo then a ramshackle **goat farm**. Angling right the track crosses a streambed – you can cross via a footbridge in the wetter months – then reaches a fork. Here turn right and follow the track, now flanked by hedgerows, steeply on upwards.

Reaching open ground the track passes well to the left of a ruined farm as views open out west across the Guadiaro valley. Levelling for a short distance it then climbs again, passing another farm building with a large water deposit then a second farmhouse fronted by a drystone wall. The track levels as it runs past a GR141 marker post then passes through a grey metal gate (which may be open).

At the next fork bear right, sticking to the main track. Angling left and descending the track crosses a streambed then arcs right and climbs once again. ▸

Continuing along the main track, following GR141 waymarking, a ruined farm comes into sight as you pass by more magnificent old gall oaks. Angling right across a streambed the track climbs again as it passes beneath power lines. Reaching the top of the rise, and another GR marker post, you reach a fork.

Here, cutting right away from the main track, you cross a shallow, concreted water channel. The track runs on, more or less parallel to the Río Guadiaro, as you cross a swathe of hillside where there's evidence of the forest fire that swept through some 10 years ago. The track passes once more beneath power lines, now descending. At a point where it loops left, to your right you'll spot a signboard atop a bluff. ▸

After passing between tumbledown gateposts the track runs up to the ruined farmhouse of **La Casa del Conde** (**3hr 25min**). Here bear hard right to reach a GR marker post then angle left, directly downhill, to a second post. Here, turning left, you pick up a narrow path which crosses a tumbledown wall then descends through thick stands of broom. Crossing a second wall the path zigzags more steeply down, at one point via steps hewn out of the rock. Dropping down across a second section of rocks, where there are wire handrails, you cross the **Puente de los Alemanes** beyond which a low-ceilinged **tunnel** leads you to the gorge's western flank.

In the valley to your west the river and railway line come into view as the track runs past some magnificent gall oaks, (*Quercus faginea*).

It's worth diverting down to the signboard marked 'Canyón de las Buitreras' for a great view south towards the gorge's narrowest section.

The Puente de los Alemanes **bridge** was part of a six-kilometre water conduit that channelled water down to the hydro-electric power station at El Colmenar. The bridge was built by a Belgian company in 1918 which somewhere down the line was said to have been German.

After 5m beyond the tunnel angle left up a narrow path which climbs very steeply, marked by cairns and standing stones. Reaching the ridgetop the path bears left and runs close to the western side of the **Canyón de las Buitreras**. Descending via a series of steps made from railway sleepers you reach a *mirador* (viewing point) opposite a narrow ledge. This is a magnificent spot to break for a picnic and observe the comings and goings of the vultures.

Beyond the mirador the path arcs right before resuming its former course. Arcing once more left it descends, now looser underfoot, in a series of loops towards the river. ◀ Running on a southerly course the path leads up

At the point where the path levels it's possible to cut left through the undergrowth to a number of beautiful bathing spots where you can dive from the rocks.

The Río Guadiaro close to Las Buitreras de El Colmenar

a flight of steps beyond which you cross a narrow foot-bridge. Returning to the river's edge it soon angles up across the hillside once again. Passing beneath a metal wire then dropping down a flight of steps you reach a paved road by the old HEP station.

Crossing the race that once funnelled water down to the station's turbines maintain your course past a line of eucalyptus trees to reach the first houses of El Colmenar. Passing house no. 20 the road bears left then, bearing left again, reaches a junction. Turn right and continue parallel to the railway past a children's play area then Mesón Las Flores to reach the square of **El Colmenar** and an ornate fountain supported by four cast-concrete horses (**5hr**).

EL COLMENAR (POPULATION 711, ALTITUDE 244M)

El Colmenar seen from the east

El Colmenar owes its existence to the Algeciras to Ronda railway which was constructed by an Anglo-Spanish company at the end of the 19th century. The village is also known locally as Estación de Gaucín. Once the railway was completed in 1892 work began on a hydro-electric power station which is located just north of the station: you pass it at the end Day 15.

Steam trains ran along the valley until 1926 before diesel locomotives were introduced while recent works were carried out so that larger and faster trains can use the line. The journey through the mountains to Ronda is among the most beautiful in Europe and was featured in a recent BBC series *Great Continental Railway Journeys*.

The village lies within the municipality of Cortes de la Frontera, at the heart of the Parque Natural de los Alcornocales which encompasses one of the largest extensions of cork oak (*Quercus suber*) forest in Europe. Thickly wooded hillsides stretch out to the south, east and west of the village while to its north lies the extraordinary Buitreras de El Colmenar, a canyon with sheer sides which rise

100m above the river Guadiaro. You walk along the rim of the canyon on Day 15. The gorge is home to a colony of griffon vultures whence its name Las Buitreras or 'Vulture Colony'. There are beautiful rock pools along the gorge where even in midsummer the waters of the Guadiaro run icy cold. The village and surrounding forests are home to a colourful, multi-ethnic community which includes organic farmers and holistic therapists, while its bars and restaurants have a laid-back yet cosmopolitan feel.

Recommended accommodation

Hotel Buitreras €
www.hotellasbuitreras.com
Simple hotel just west of the railway station.

Casa Rural AhORA €
www.casaruralahora.com
Riverside B&B with excellent breakfasts and dinners using organic produce.

Contacts
Ayuntamiento: www.cortesdelafrontera.es
Taxi: nearest taxi in Gaucín, José María 600 294 138

The station platform at El Colmenar

Start	The small square, next to the fountain with 4 horses, El Colmenar
Distance	25km
Ascent/Descent	670m/815m
Grade	Difficult
Time	7hr
Map	IGN 1:50000 Cortes de la Frontera 1064 & Jimena de la Frontera 1071
Refreshments	None en route
Advice	The middle section of the stage is becoming overgrown in parts, so be sure to have long trousers or gaiters in your day pack.

The challenging sixteenth day of the Coast to Coast Walk offers ample recompense for the effort you'll expend. The walk leads through a wild and rugged swathe of sierra where the likelihood of spotting eagles and deer is excellent while your destination, Jimena de la Frontera, numbers among Andalucía's most beautiful villages.

Leaving El Colmenar a steep path leads up to the village's arboretum. Next comes an easy section of track walking as you skirt the eastern flank of El Robledal, high above the Río Guadiaro. Crossing the upper reaches of the Arroyo Garganta de Casilla you're faced with a steep climb through the forest to the highest point of the stage where you link up with the GR7.

On a clear day, on the long descent to Jimena, you're treated to amazing views south to Gibraltar, the Bay of Algeciras and across the Strait to the Moroccan Rif.

The stage begins just to the south of the railway station of El Colmenar in a paved square next to a fountain supported by four cast-concrete horses. Leave the square by crossing the railway line and passing right of the Unicaja bank. Passing right of house no. 31 climb to the top of

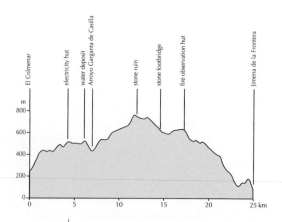

the street then angle right then left up Calle Semillero. Passing a pylon the street arcs right then reaches the **MA-512** which connects El Colmenar and Cortes de la Frontera.

Angle right across the road past a 6T weight limit sign then climb a path which soon meets the MA-512 once again. Cross the road and continue up a steep dirt track to reach the road once again. Follow the road as it arcs hard left. A few metres past a **Casa Forestal** with twin blue bollards, where to your right there's a sign for **Arboreto de El Colmenar**, cut left away from the MA-512 up a steep, tarmac road.

> The **arboretum** at El Colmenar dates back to the early years of the 20th century when more than a hundred different species of eucalyptus were planted as part of a study to see which trees were best suited for paper production. Most species still remain.

At the point where the track arcs left keep straight ahead and go through a wire-and-post gate. Continue up a narrow path, marked by cairns and marker posts,

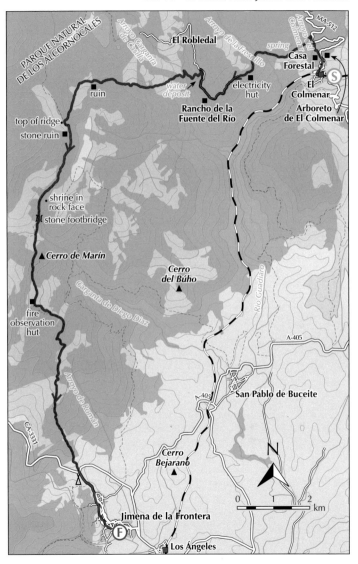

that climbs through the eucalypti. Bearing left the path reaches a flatter area and a forestry track. Bear right along this stony track which soon angles right and runs up to the MA-512. Turn left and go along the road which shortly arcs right. At 75m beyond this bend, opposite a stone and ceramic sign for 'Puerto', turn left to follow a broad dirt track (**20min**).

The track soon loops left and crosses a bridge. Contouring round the mountain it runs past a spring then passes above a ruined farm. Reaching a fork just beyond a concrete inspection hut continue straight along the main track. Soon you pass above a house with a pool tucked in among the oaks.

Passing another spring the track loops across an oleander-lined streambed via a concrete bridge then runs past a white farm shed then an **electricity hut** flanked by repeater masts. Climbing gently across the eastern flank of **El Robledal** the track reaches more open ground where views open out to the south. Here the track angles right, still ascending gently, before passing a cattle grid.

Adopting a southwesterly course the track passes beneath power lines. Some 150m after passing a water deposit with a hatch on its roof turn left off the track at a cairn (**1hr 20min**) and drop down a narrower forestry track.

Looping steeply down the track reaches a clearing among the oaks. Here maintain your course. The track becomes clearer once again, marked by cairns, before it descends to a junction with a track that cuts across the hillside from **Rancho de la Fuente del Río** (marked on your map though not visible during the walk) to the valley floor. Here angle right. After crossing a streambed the track angles left then crosses the larger stream of the **Arroyo Garganta de Casilla** via stepping stones (**1hr 55min**).

Having crossed the streambed bear left and continue along the track for 200m looking for a cairn to your right. Here cut right up a track which climbs steeply through the heather and broom. The track levels and crosses a streambed, just beyond which another track comes in to

Centenarian gall oak close to the Arroyo Garganta de Casilla

meet yours from the left. Here maintain your course, still climbing steeply, shortly passing once again beneath the power lines.

Eventually the track levels, descends gently, then climbs once again, now deeply eroded in parts. The track crosses a rocky streambed by a leaning cork oak (*Quercus suber*). Bearing left then back to the right after some 125m you'll spot a tumbledown stone wall over to your left. Here leave the track by a cairn (**2hr 50min**).

Head directly up and over the stone wall then cut left and follow the wall round the outside of a flattish field, still looking for cairns. On the far side of the field, just before reaching a ruined, overgrown corral, angle left through a gap in the wall then drop down and cross a streambed. Just beyond the streambed pass left of a huge old oak and continue along a narrow path, indistinct at this stage, which runs parallel to a wooden-posted fence, and beyond it a stream, which is over to your left.

Using the GPX track of the route could be reassuring on this section.

For the best part of an hour, until you reach the top of the rise, look for cairns and fading green paint splashes: the path is constantly braiding on this section. ◄

You cross another streambed after which the path bears left and continues to climb: occasionally you'll see the wooden-posted fence down to your left. The path becomes looser and sandier underfoot. Crossing another streambed then climbing steeply the path bears hard left and runs closer to the fence. Shortly, just past a point where the path has been deeply eroded, you cross a streambed. Here the path divides. Keep right, following the clearer path, which runs on across a flatter area.

Climbing once again the path soon angles left, through the heather, to run close once again to the side of the stream and fence. Cairns still guide you upwards past huge sandstone boulders and cork oaks. Having crossed a deeper streambed the path divides. Here, bearing right then passing through a gap in a tumbledown stone wall, you come to a more open area where the forest has been felled and where immediately ahead of you'll spot a tumbledown **ruin** (**2hr 35min**).

Pass just right of the ruin then angle slightly right to pick up an indistinct track which climbs steeply, still more or less parallel to the stream which is over to your left. After crossing two of its tributaries the track loops left then crosses the stream: still you'll see the wooden-posted fence, and an old stone wall, over to your left.

Keep heading on up between the fence to your left and with the stream now to your right. The track, now much clearer, levels then angles left before climbing steeply on towards the **top of the ridge**. Reaching more open ground maintain your course for some 100m then angle left away from the track towards a low stone wall and a trig point marked 'C2C' in green paint. Passing through a gap in the wall you reach the top of the ridge (**3hr 55min**).

Angling left, after 25m you reach a sandy track. Here branch left. The track descends, then 20 metres before it loops left towards a black metal gate reaches a sign for 'GR7 Ubrique 5.30hr, Jimena 4.30 hrs'. ◄ Here cut right down a broad track.

You'll need far less time than indicated by the sign.

Passing above a **stone ruin** you reach a point where the track bears hard right. Here carry straight on along a less clearly defined track which passes left of a huge rock. Crossing a streambed continue past a chain slung between two metal posts. Continuing along the track for 450m you reach another GR7 signpost for 'Jimena de la Frontera 4 hrs'.

Here branch left along a narrow path. It crosses a streambed then climbs gently as the countryside opens out. Passing another GR post the path leads you through a wire-and-post gate. Some 50m beyond the gate your path merges with a broad track which bears right then after a few metres divides. Here branch left and follow the track downhill for 100m.

Some 20m before reaching a drainage channel turn along a narrow path. Passing a GR7 marker post, the path descends parallel to a streambed which it shortly crosses then runs down through thick undergrowth, close to the stream's left bank. Crossing back to its right bank it then arcs left. After some 300m you pass a small **shrine** to

Shrine in the cliff face passed on the descent towards Jimena de la Frontera

the Virgin in a rockface to your left, directly above the stream. At 35m beyond the shrine the path crosses back to the stream's left bank then, descending still, cuts back a final time to its right bank.

Reaching more open ground the path becomes less distinct as it threads its way through clumps of ferns. Passing another GR7 post for 'Jimena de la Frontera 3.30hrs' the path bears right then crosses a **stone footbridge**. Looping left it widens to become a track which continues to descend. The track soon runs across a more open tract of land then reaches a broader track. Here, following a marker post for 'Jimena 3.15hrs' bear left.

To the east the villages of San Pablo de Buceite and Casares come into view and, as you climb higher, Gibraltar and the Moroccan Rif.

You shortly pass signs for 'Monte Majada del Lobo' and 'Montes de Jimena de la Frontera'. Crossing a cattle grid you pass through a green metal gate (**4hr 55min**).

The track soon passes through another wire-and-post gate in a stone wall with another sign 'Coto Privado de Caza'. Beyond the gate it loops right, merging with another track, now heading along a sandy ridgetop. ◄

Reaching a **fire observation hut** the track divides. Here angle left at a sign 'Jimena 2.30hrs' and continue down a stony track. After descending for 100m you pass a GR post to the right of the track. Continue down the track for another 100m then cut right up an indistinct path which passes a second GR7 post before running up to a wire-and-post gate in a low stone wall. Beyond the gate angle left and make your way down through the rocks, sticking close to the stone wall, to reach a broad sandy track.

Bear left along the track which loops right and descends through oaks and pines; a fence soon runs just to your left. Looping left you pass a sign for 'Depósitos'. ◄ After passing signs for 'Monte Benazainilla' then 'Mirador' – it's worth cutting in left for some 25m to take in the views – then a second sign for 'Monte Benazainilla' the track levels as you reach a GR7 sign 'Jimena 1.15hrs'. Here bear left away from the track and go through a galvanised metal gate. Beyond the gate continue down a stony, eroded track through a stand of cork oaks.

Jimena, and its hilltop castle, comes into view.

You soon pass through a second galvanised metal gate beyond which you should bear left down an indistinct path which runs towards another marker post, descending parallel to a wall which is over to your left. ▸ Passing through a small gate to one side of a larger green metal gate you reach a track (**6hr 25min**).

Turn right then after 20m cut left at a sign 'Jimena 30mins'. Go through another gate then continue down a narrow path between two walls. The path becomes cobbled then descends to the CA-3331. Cross the road and head straight on towards the village.

Passing a **campsite** then a series of exercise machines angle right, away from the road, then after 15m bear left along a paved path which passes a metal sculpture before meeting the road once again. Reaching a fork take the road to the right, following a sign 'Centro Ciudad'. At the end of the street bear right then left and continue down Calle Llana. At the end of the street turn left then immediately right past a children's play area. The street climbs then levels.

Jimena de la Frontera seen from the east

If in doubt, take the closest path to the wall.

Reaching a 'No Entry' sign bear left down Calle Loba. At the next junction turn right and go along Calle Cruz del Rincón, take the next left along Caminete del Luna then turn right down Calle Consuelo. Some 50m beyond Hostal El Anon turn left and go along Calle Jincalete then right down Calle San Sebastian to reach La Plaza de la Constitución (**7hr**).

JIMENA DE LA FRONTERA (POPULATION 9756, ALTITUDE 90M)

Jimena de la Frontera's Calle San Sebastian with its castle visible high above

Lying close to the point where two valleys cut through the final reaches of the southern mountains towards the Mediterranean, the lands in and around Jimena have been populated since prehistoric times: Palaeolithic rock paintings were found at the Laja Alta site west of the village along with burial sites close to the Hozgarganta river. Phoenician coins were discovered where the present castle stands while during the Roman period a sizeable *urbis* (city) called Oba developed which was of sufficient importance to have minted its own coins.

After their arrival in Spain in 711 the Moors were quick to establish a settlement atop the hill where the castle now stands which they named Xemena.

Initially ruled by Benimerin Berbers the village later came under the sway of the Nasrid sultans of Granada when it became an important outpost of its western border, thus its de la Frontera epithet. The town was captured by the Christians in 1431, then retaken by the Moors 20 years later before being definitively reconquered in 1456.

Jimena was to live a brief moment of importance during a series of conflicts with Britain leading on from the signing of the Treaty of Utrecht in 1713, when a foundry was constructed to one side of the Hozgarganta river for the manufacture of cannon balls: many were fired across the water during the Siege of Gibraltar in the late 18th century. The old foundry now houses an excellent B&B (see Recommended accommodation, Jimena).

The town would later suffer extensive damage during La Guerra de la Independencía (aka The Peninsular War) at which time its municipal archives were destroyed by the Napoleonic troops.

Today Jimena has something of the feel of a crossroads between the coast and the mountains to the north while the countryside west of the village is among the wildest in Andalucía: the region was long a favoured hunting ground of royals and their nobles. The creation of Los Alcornocales Natural Park has brought rural tourism to the area while the arrival of many foreign residents – they number about a tenth of the present population – has boosted the local economy.

Recommended accommodation

Casa Henrietta €€
www.casahenrietta.com
A beautifully decorated and warmly welcoming hotel with great views from most rooms.

Hostal El Anon €€
www.hostalanon.com
Characterful hostel with rooftop plunge pool. Popular with walking groups.

El Estanque y El Almendro €€
www.elestanqueyelalmendro.com
Riverside B&B housed within the old artillery factory just beneath the village and with organically sourced meals.

Contacts

Ayuntamiento: **www.jimenadelafrontera.es**
Taxi: David 607 383 590

DAY 17
Jimena de la Frontera to Castillo de Castellar

Start	The bell tower in La Plaza de la Constitución, Jimena de la Frontera
Distance	22.1km
Ascent/Descent	285m/125m
Grade	Medium
Time	5hr 40min
Map	IGN 1:50000 Jimena de la Frontera 1071 & La Línea de la Concepción 1075
Refreshments	None en route

Although much of the seventeenth leg of the Coast to Coast Walk is by way of the flat valley floor of the Guadiaro valley, this is still a reasonably challenging, full-day walk.

Leaving Jimena you drop steeply downhill then cross the Hozgarganta river. After a short section of tarmac, a broad dirt track leads you southwards, sticking close to the Algeciras to Ronda railway line. There are few passing trains and the hedgerows to either side of the track are home to abundant birdlife.

Eventually you cut west across the railway line then follow a steep, cobbled track up across densely forested hillsides to the citadel fortress of Castillo de Castellar. This eerily beautiful enclave numbers among the architectural and historical highlights of the Coast to Coast Walk.

The route is marked with GR7 waymarking but many of the signs are fading, fallen or damaged.

The stage begins next to the bell tower in Jimena's Plaza de la Constitución. Leave the square at its top, left corner and head up Calle San Sebastian following signs for 'Castillo/Fortaleza'. Take the first turning left and head along to the end of Calle Jincaleta. Here angle right across a small square, turn left down Calle La Vaca then bear right into Chorro de la Calle. Pass a fountain and at

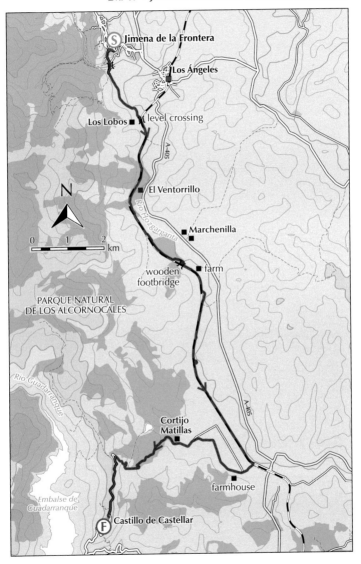

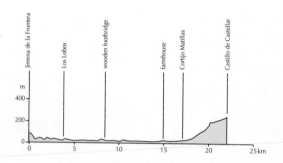

the end of the road drop down a flight of brick steps to a tarmac road. Here turn right and drop down the hill following a row of street lamps. After passing by a sign 'Sendero Río Hozgarganta' the road merges with another then crosses a **bridge** over the Río Hozgarganta.

After 300m, where the road bears right, cut left along a dirt track following a sign for 'Rancho Los Lobos' and a GR7 marker post 'Castellar 6hrs'. The track runs south between fences. Passing the entrance to **Los Lobos** the track crosses a **level crossing** beyond which you pass a sign for 'Marchenilla'. The track runs on between hedgerows, just left of the railway, before reaching a junction with a broader track where, in front of you, is a rusting black metal gate (**50min**).

Stick to your same course, following GR7 waymarking and a sign for 'La Bordalla', still parallel to the railway. Soon you pass by (though don't cross) a level crossing. The terrain becomes more wooded as the track runs on past the twin-eagled entrance gate of **El Ventorrillo** then a couple more single-storey houses before it passes by a second level crossing. Angling hard right (**1hr 40min**) the track runs towards a third level crossing. Just before you reach it branch left, maintaining your course, following a GR7 sign 'Castellar, 4.45hrs'.

The track narrows, running on between hedgerows, then descends to cross a streambed via a concreted ford

Grazing horses close to the Ronda to Algeciras railway line

where, to your right, is a damaged footbridge. Beyond the ford the track adopts its former course, just left of the tracks. Soon it runs up to meet a track that runs up towards the railway line.

Here bear left – don't cross the railway line – along a broad track, parallel to a fence made of wooden railway sleepers. After 200m the track swings left. Here maintain your course along a narrower, sandier track following a GR7 sign for 'Castellar 14.5km'. After crossing a streambed the track runs on just left of the railway before narrowing to become a footpath which descends to a **wooden footbridge**. Having crossed the footbridge you reach a track. Here, bearing round to the right, you pass a rusting level crossing sign. Just before you reach the railway track and a 'Stop' sign angle once more left and head on, parallel to the track which is again just to your right.

Soon you pass the entrance to a small **farm** with flowerpots on its stone pillars. The track runs along the edge of an enormous field, passes through a wire-and-post gate, then bearing left then right, passes through a leafy copse. Running on along the edge of another large

Eroded footpath beside the railway line

field you reach a track cutting left towards the Jimena to Algeciras road. Here continue straight ahead, along the edge of another vast field, to a wire-and-post gate (**2hr 30min**).

Go through the gate then cross a streambed. Running on just left of the railway the track narrows to become a path. After cutting along the edge of a field it widens again, angles left, then descends towards the river. Just before reaching the river it arcs sharply right then climbs, slightly overgrown at this stage, to reach a wire-and-post gate.

Go through the gate then turn right then left along a track, sticking to the edge of a field. Carry straight on past a 'Stop' sign, holding your course to the far end of the field. Here the path bears right through hedgerows then runs on beside the railway line as you pass by a plantation of young pine trees.

Passing through another wire-and-post gate the track runs on along the edge of another huge field, parallel to a line of water hydrants as the countryside opens out.

Passing by two level crossings – but not crossing them – Castillo de Castellar comes into sight over to your right on a high hilltop. Eventually you reach a junction with a broad track (**3hr 45min**).

Here turn right at a sign for 'GR7 Castellar 7.1kms' then pass over a level crossing to reach the west side of the railway line. Continue straight ahead, ignoring a track that angles left, parallel to the track. Having crossed a bridge the track bears right then reaches a fork. Take the left fork, sticking to the main track which soon passes a **farmhouse** then, arcing left, runs along the edge of a vast field where it begins to climb. Castellar again comes into view. You pass abandoned farm buildings to the left of the track then **Cortijo Matillas** to the right with a sign on its gates 'Coto Privado de Caza'.

The track, now cobbled and deeply eroded, angles left and crosses a stone bridge. Climbing on across a thickly wooded hillside between two fences the track leads through a wire-and-post gate. Here continue on your same course, passing right of a GR7 marker post. The track eventually passes by a marker post pointing left down a narrow path. Ignoring this turn, after a few metres cobbles give way to tarmac.

La Plaza de la Posada

Huge views open out to the east and southeast towards Gibraltar and, on clear days, to the Moroccan Rif.

Continue along the tarmac road, ignoring turnings to its right and left. ◄ After the track runs past the village cemetery Castillo de Castellar comes into view. Passing the first houses of the village you reach the entrance to the hilltop citadel of **Castillo de Castellar** next to Bar El Cortijo. Here turn right up a cobbled street which angles left before passing beneath an arch. Cutting right then bearing left beneath a second arch you reach Plaza la Posada (**5hr 40min**).

CASTILLO DE CASTELLAR (POPULATION 103, ALTITUDE 244M)

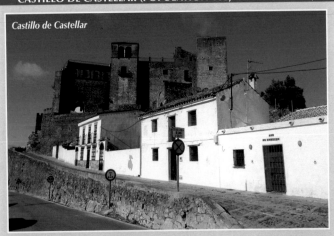

Castillo de Castellar

There are few places in Andalucía so enigmatically evocative nor with such a fascinating history as Castillo de Castellar. The high pinnacle of rock on which it stands has long been a site of strategic importance as testified by Roman and Visgothic remains found within the present castle and the *calzada romana* (old Roman footpath) which you follow at the beginning of Day 18. Occupied soon after the conquest of Jebel Tariq – present-day Gibraltar – it was in the 13th century that the Moors built the citadel fortress which today numbers among the best preserved in Andalucía. It speaks of an age when a line of fortresses stretching north towards Ronda marked the boundary between Catholic and Islamic Andalucía.

The Reconquest of the village by Juan Arias de Saavedra was to usher in several centuries of virtual serfdom for the villagers. The management of the vast *latifundia* (huge estates, some of which date from the Reconquest) surrounding the settlement – it passed into the hands of the Medinaceli family soon after – remained a peculiar anachronism as late as the 1960s. It was then that Franco's ministers built Nuevo Castellar in the valley next to the railway line and distributed land among the villagers which was irrigated by the newly created Guadarranque reservoir. After the villagers moved out of the castillo a hippy community moved in and for years Castellar became a kind of state-within-a-state and synonymous with drugs and rock and roll.

Nowadays things are less radical and the opening of the Hotel El Alcázar, along with a number of self-catering houses, has attracted a different type of visitor. A few of the original hippies are still around running bars and arty-crafty shops: they have fascinating stories to tell.

In the mid-1970s, at the time of a dispute between the villagers and the Almoraima estate, Felipe González intervened on behalf of the village. He was thanked for his efforts with the gift of a house within the walls of the castle and is still an occasional visitor. Every year in July, coinciding with the full moon, Castellar stages a flamenco festival in the Plaza del Salvador, while the first weekend in August there's more music on the night of La Velada del Divino Salvador

Recommended accommodation

La Posada Travellers Inn €–€€
678 626 550 or 625 533 642
Two lovely rooms, good food, run by young, English-speaking hosts.

Hotel El Alcázar €€
www.tugasa.com
Hotel housed within the old castle with restaurant, bar and rooms-with-a-view.

Recommended accommodation close to the village
Hotel Convento La Almoraima €€
www.laalmoraimahotel.com
Stylish rooms within a beautiful 18th-century convent within the vast estate of La Almoraima.

Contacts
Ayuntamiento: **www.castellar.es**
Tourist Office: 956 236 887
Taxi: nearest taxi in San Pablo 649 348 077

DAY 18

Castillo de Castellar to Los Barrios

Start	Plaza la Posada, Castillo de Castellar
Distance	24.5km
Ascent/Descent	340m/565m
Grade	Medium/Difficult
Time	6hr 45min
Map	IGN 1:50000 La Línea de la Concepción 1075
Refreshments	Bars and restaurants in Nuevo Castellar and Estación de San Roque

Day 18 of the Coast to Coast Walk leads down from Castillo de Castellar to the floor of the Guadiaro valley before running on south towards Los Barrios.

At the beginning of the stage you follow an ancient footpath known locally as La Calzada then the old road which cuts through the oak forest of the estate of La Almoraima (see Castillo de Castellar section, Day 17).

Arriving at the outskirts of Castellar de la Frontera you continue parallel to the railway via broad farm tracks. Eventually you cross the railway line where you meet the A-405 where a cycle path leads you to the outskirts of Estación de San Roque.

You're now faced with 5km of road walking, the longest stretch of tarmac on the Coast to Coast Walk – it's impossible to avoid due to the closure to the public of footpaths that cross the Almoraima estate – as you climb to a ridgetop high above Los Barrios. From here you descend to the village along narrow tracks from where there are sweeping vistas out west to the Bay of Algeciras and across the town to the forested slopes of the Sierra de Ojén.

Exit the square of Plaza la Posada in Castillo de Castellar beneath an arch. Bearing right pass beneath two more arches then continue along a cobbled path parallel to the battlements. The path loops left then right before reaching a white house to your left. Here turn left down a

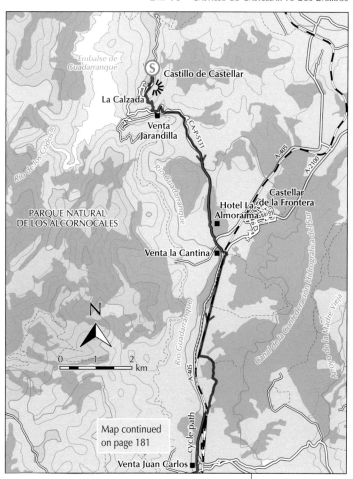

Map continued
on page 181

narrow path which descends between a group of single-storey houses. Reaching the **CA-P-5131** follow it left for 30m then turn right at a GR7 sign for 'Los Barrios, 9hrs 40mins'. Here you pick up the Roman path of **La Calzada** which shortly passes a **mirador** (viewing point). Reaching

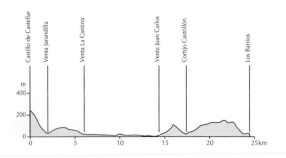

a junction angle left, following the path steeply down past sandstone boulders to reach the CA-P-5131.

Turn left and go along the road for 150m then, just as the road bears sharply right, cut right down a narrow path which descends through thick vegetation, crosses a stream, then runs back up to the road.

One of Castillo de Castellar's eastern battlements

Bearing right along the side of the road you pass **Venta Jarandilla** then after 100m, as the road bears left, reach a junction next to a 'Stop' sign and a GR7 marker post. Here angle right away from the CA-P-5131 for 5m then bear left along a rutted, disused road which runs gently uphill, parallel to the new road which is to your left. Running beneath a bridge the road angles right then meets the CA-P-5131 again. Turn left and continue along the left side of the road. After passing the build-ings of the **Hotel la Almoraima** you reach a roundabout (**1hr 40min**).

Bear right along the **A-405** following signs for 'San Roque' and 'Algeciras' past a depot where cork is stored then **Venta La Cantina**. Beyond the *venta* (roadside res-taurant) the road arcs right then crosses a bridge. Just beyond the bridge turn left at signs for 'Ayuntamiento' and 'Hotel Castellar'. Cross the railway line and head straight on. Some 15m beyond a sign marking the entrance of Castellar de la Frontera turn right and go along a broad

Fallen oak on the Roman footpath beneath Castillo de Castellar

179

track which soon angles right then adopts a course parallel to the railway line, which is now to your right. Continue due south past groves of loquat, avocado and citrus trees, ignoring two tracks which cut right towards level crossings.

Eventually the track angles 90 degrees left, away from the railway (ignore a less distinct track which continues straight ahead) then passes beneath a building on a low rise. Passing by two sets of farm gates you reach a junction. Here cut right through a farm gate beyond which you pass just left of a ramshackle shed.

After 400m the track runs towards a sliding, green metal gate, to the left of which is a breeze-block wall. At 10m before the gate bear left along a sandy track which leads to a wire-and-post gate. Go through the gate then follow an indistinct track which angles right, parallel to a fence which is to your right. ◀ After 500m the track angles left across the field, passes beneath overhead cables then bears right along the edge of a small lake.

Passing through a wire-and-post gate continue across a smaller field on a course parallel to a metal fence, the A-405 and the railway line. Reaching a 'Stop' sign and a level crossing, pass through a rickety gate then cross the railway track to reach another 'Stop' sign. Passing through a gap to the right of a blue metal gate you reach the A-405 (**3hr**).

Cut left and follow a **cycle path** along the left side of the road for 600m then cross the road and continue south along a slip road following a sign for 'San Roque, A-405R2'. Passing **Venta Juan Carlos** you reach a GR7 marker post for 'Los Barrios 6.25 hrs' to your right.

Here turn right and go along the **CA-9207**. The road soon crosses the Río Guadarranque. Just beyond a **horse stables** turn left and go along a broad dirt track. At the end of the track, just before a sliding metal gate, turn right, go through a wire-and-post gate then continue along a straight, causeway-like road. ◀

Passing through another wire-and-post gate you meet the CA-9207 once again. Cross the road then pass through a third wire-and-post gate and continue up a

In spring and summer you'll see dozens of white storks (Ciconia ciconia) nesting atop the pylons which run south down the valley.

You'll often see black kites (Milvus migrans) perched on the telegraph wire that runs along the road's left-hand side.

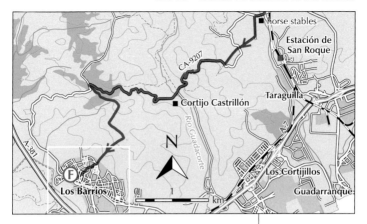

rougher, tarmac road. Passing through another gate you meet once more with the CA-9207. Here cut right and follow the road on upwards. Steel yourself for a little over 5km of road walking. ▸

After following a looping section of road you descend and pass a junction with a broad track where the GR7 turns right. Here, continue along the CA-9207. After crossing a bridge you pass **Cortijo Castrillón** as the road begins to gently ascend. Eventually, after passing by two tracks cutting left to the municipal rubbish dump (it's out of sight) the road loops left past a junction marked 'C.M. Sur de Europa'. Bearing left, following a sign 'Los Barrios' for 20m, cut left away from the CA-9207 and pass through a metal gate (**5hr 15min**).

Beyond the gate, continuing along a sandy track, you pass a signboard 'El Alcornocal de Palmares'. Passing through a wire-and-post gate the sandy track climbs, levels, then passes through a red metal gate. Reaching a pylon angle right and drop downhill following a line of pylons. As the rutted track levels you pass a sign 'El Palmar del Cerro Marcelo' then pass through a stile to the right of a wire-and-post gate. The track improves as it arcs left and runs along a ridgetop where it passes a group of houses surrounded by high hedges. Continue

On a clear day, looking south, you'll see the peak of Jebel Musa in Morocco rising high above the Strait.

181

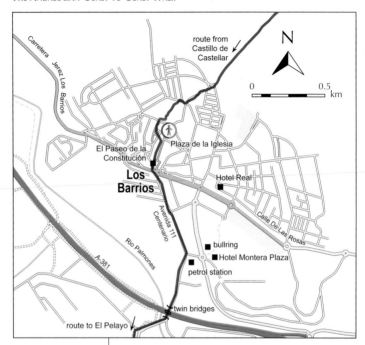

along the ridgetop then follow the track as it bears right and descends steeply to the outskirts of **Los Barrios** where you reach a roundabout.

Cross the roundabout and continue along Camino de las Haciendas. Passing a children's playground you reach a junction. Here bear right following signs for 'Ayuntamiento' and 'Iglesia de San Isidro Labrador'. When you reach the second of two pedestrian crossings cut left down Calle Nueva. At the end of the street continue straight on past a metal bollard then bear right along a narrow street. Just beyond house no. 7 turn right. Reaching a chemist's angle left along Calle Águilas to reach the pretty, palm-lined square of La Plaza de la Iglesia (**6hr 45min**).

LOS BARRIOS (POPULATION 22,311, ALTITUDE 24M)

Los Barrios seen from the north

Lying at the confluence of the rivers Palmones, Cañas and Guadarranque and to one side of a major corridor through the mountains between the Mediterranean Sea and the Atlantic Ocean the area in and around Los Barrios has seen many comings and goings over the millennia. Until recently it was believed that the present town dated from the early 18th century when Spaniards, ousted from Gibraltar by the British, formed a small settlement here. Recent archaeological studies have pushed its origins much further back: Palaeolithic remains have been discovered as well as evidence of an earlier Moorish *alquería* (from Arabic, meaning 'a group of farm buildings').

The village's municipality is one of the largest in Andalucía and includes the fishing village of Palmones as well as a large swathe of Los Alcornocales Natural Park. The area that lies to the south of the village is subject to both Mediterranean and Atlantic climatic patterns. These twin influences have given rise to a unique microclimate, one which nurtures the unusual flora of its narrow streams or *canutos*: you cross a number of them on Day 19. The region's unique flora attracted the renowned English botanist Betty Molesworth Allen to the town. She lived and studied there for more than 40 years, and a park in the town now bears her name. Her book *Wildflowers of Southern Spain* remains a classic botanical tome. Los Barrios is rich in natural resources: fish from the sea and fruit and vegetables from its irrigated valley floor, as well as beef from the cattle which are raised on the hillsides surrounding the village. *Toros bravos* – fighting bulls – are also bred in the area and the town forms part of the recently created Ruta del Toro. The vast swathes of forested hillsides that lie west of the town stand in stark contrast to the urban sprawl of the Bay of Algeciras, home to the Acerinox steelworks and a huge oil refinery, as well as being one of the largest bunkering points in the Mediterranean.

Recommended accommodation
Hotel Real €€
www.hotelreallosbarrios.es
A modern 1-star hotel in the town centre with a popular restaurant.

Hotel Montera Plaza €€
www.hotelemontera.com
Brash 4-star hotel at the edge of the town with quiet, comfortable rooms.

Contacts
Ayuntamiento: **www.losbarrios.es**
Taxi: main rank 956 574 444 or Pedro 608 548 354

*Gibraltar and the Bay
of Algeciras seen from
close to Los Barrios*

DAY 19

Los Barrios to El Pelayo

Start	La Plaza de la Iglesia, Los Barrios
Distance	25.5km
Ascent/Descent	575m/350m
Grade	Medium/Difficult
Time	7hr 5min
Map	IGN 1:50000 La Línea de la Concepción 1075, Tarifa 1077 & Algeciras 1078
Refreshments	None en route

This long and averagely challenging stage leads south from Los Barrios to link in with a forestry track which loops up and over the thickly wooded hillsides of the Sierra de Ojén. The area is home to abundant wildlife and contains pristine tracts of ancient woodland which have been given doubly protected status within the Natural Park of Los Alcornocales.

As you climb from Los Barrios vast views open out across the Bay of Algeciras towards Gibraltar and, on a clear day, to the distant peaks of the Moroccan Rif. After the long ascent during the first half of the stage the latter section is plain sailing as you descend towards the Strait and the roadside settlement of El Pelayo.

The wild beauty of this section of the Coast to Coast Walk belies the fact that the sprawling conurbation of Algeciras lies only a few kilometres to the east.

The stage begins in front of a fountain with twin sculpted heads in La Plaza de la Iglesia at the heart of Los Barrios, in front of the *ayuntamiento* (town hall). With your back to the fountain angle 45 degrees left and exit the square between house no. 6 and house no. 2 down a narrow alley. Reaching a junction turn right and go along Los Barrios' main shopping street to reach the lively square of El Paseo de la Constitución. Continue on past a bandstand then turn left. After 20m you come to a roundabout.

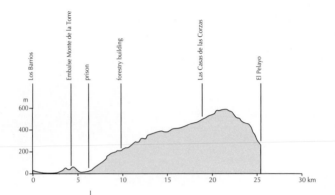

Here turn right and go along Avenida III Centenario. Cross to the other side of the road, bear right, then follow a pedestrian walkway parallel to the avenue and a line of palm trees.

Reaching a roundabout at the avenue's far end pass to the right of a petrol station, and continue along a broad street with a pavement to its right which shortly passes beneath the **twin bridges** of the A-381 motorway. The road bears right then crosses a footbridge over the Río de las Cañas. Beyond the bridge follow a sandy path that runs along the side of the **CA-9209**.

Reaching a junction angle slightly right past a sign 'Corredor Verde Dos Bahias' then continue, parallel to the CA-9209. After crossing three wooden bridges you cross a fourth, larger one, with a metal base. Here turn right at a sign 'Puerta Verde Algeciras' along a sandy track (**40min**).

Reaching a fork after 35m, angle left and continue past a helipad (it's used by the Spanish customs who control the nearby Strait) up a sandy path with fences to either side. After crossing a low rise the track descends then runs round the right side of the **Embalse Monte de la Torre**. ◄

Passing the reservoir you should be treated to the sight of hundreds of cattle egrets (*Bubulcus ibis*) perched in the trees that surround the lake. Grey herons (*Ardea cinerea*) are also a common sight.

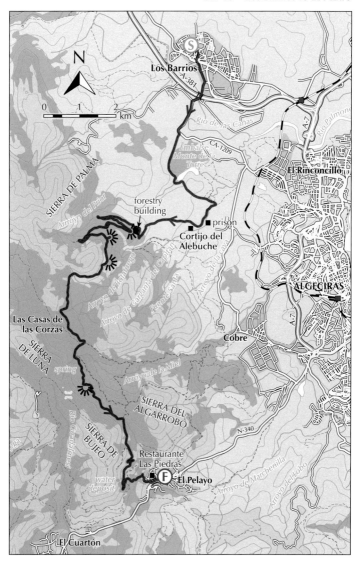

Reaching a junction, still close to the reservoir, cut left across a wooden bridge then bear left, parallel to the reservoir banks. Soon the path bears right, climbs, then crosses a rise beyond which the blue-roofed **prison** of Algeciras comes into view.

Passing between two sets of yellow posts you reach a junction with a broader track. Here turn right, pass through an opening in a post-and-rail fence, and continue past a picnic area. Fording the Arroyo de Garganta del Capitán the track runs up to another junction in front of a galvanised metal gate. Here turn right.

The track passes a ruined building then narrowing loops right and crosses the stream you forded earlier in the stage, the Arroyo de Garganta del Capitán. Bearing left you reach a gate marked 'C.A.', the entrance to **Cortijo del Acebuche**. Go through the gate then, passing between two farm sheds, follow a broad track which climbs gently across open countryside then pass through another gate with a sign 'Por Favor, Cerrar La Engarilla'. ◄

Be prepared to pass grazing cattle here. You're now following the Vereda del Mesto, an ancient drovers' path.

Gibraltar seen from the track beyond Cortijo del Acebuche

Soon you pass through another gate which marks the beginning of Finca El Galeón. The track loops steeply upwards as views open out towards the Bay of Algeciras before passing through another gate where you pass just right of a cattle grid. Resuming its upwardly mobile course the track angles hard right, passes a small white **forestry building** with a vine-covered terrace then loops on up through a swathe of mountainside where re-afforestation has taken place. Ascending you reach rockier terrain where cork oaks become more abundant. The track describes a tight hairpin then, still climbing, reaches a **mirador** (viewing point) and a sign for 'Hoyo de Don Pedro' where a damaged signboard depicts what lies before you (**3hr**).

Here the track arcs hard round to the right. Continuing its ascent, after a tight double hairpin, it adopts a southwesterly course, high above the Arroyo del Prior which cuts a deep cleft in the flank of the Sierra de la Palma. Looping sharply left you pass a section of wire-meshed retaining wall where you reach more open countryside. Crossing another cattle grid you reach a

The gate between Cortijo del Acebuche and Finca Galeón

189

This is a magnificent spot to break your journey with a stunning panoramic view of the Bay of Algeciras, Gibraltar and – on clear days – the North African coast.

second sign for 'Mirador'. You reach the **mirador** by cutting left for 70m (**4hr**). Like the earlier viewing point this one also has a signboard, this one marked 'Mirador Hoyo Don Pedro'. ◄

From the mirador continue along the track which shortly descends for a short distance, levels then climbs once more as it contours round the southeastern flank of the **Sierra de Palma**. The jagged peaks of the Cerros de los Esclarecidos are visible over to your left. Running past a third **mirador** then passing through a green gate (to the right of a larger green gate that's sometimes locked) you pass just right of another cattle grid.

Beyond the gate the track climbs gently on upwards as, over to your left, **Las Casas de las Corzas** come into view amidst a sea of green. Soon the track bears left, adopting a more southerly course, then runs past a gate with a sign 'Finca Privada: Prohibido El Paso', one of the entrances to Las Corzas. Continue along the track, with the boundary fence of Las Corzas just to your right.

Passing a galvanised metal gate the track angles right as it runs past an enclosure with a ramp for loading cattle. Soon you pass by a second gate, set in crenellated stone posts, marked 'Casa de las Corzas'. The track runs on, quite level now, as the Mediterranean to the east of Tarifa

Logs of cork oak, Quercus Suber, with Las Corzas visible in the background

comes into view. Passing another cattle grid the track widens before crossing a pretty *canuto* (streambed with an unusually diverse plant life, born of its moist, cloud forest-like climate). just beyond which you reach a **spring** just to the right of the track, at the base of a stone wall (**5hr 15min**).

The track runs past a water tank then passes across another canuto as it snakes lazily onwards, passing a picnic area with a fading signboard explaining why the area's wildlife and plants are so zealously protected.

Shortly beyond the sign the track runs past another **mirador** with a sign 'Cabecera del Río de la Miel'.

As you lose sight of Gibraltar the track crosses another cattle grid then, looping right, begins to descend: cork oaks are now interspersed with pines. ▶ Just beyond a sign marked 'Monte Algamasilla' the track arcs right, hairpins left then right, then begins to descend as you pass beneath overhead power lines. After passing a **water deposit** after 400m the track arcs hard left. Just beyond a concrete marker post marked 'Revia 340 km20' the track loops back to the right (**6hr 45min**).

Here cut left at a cairn down a path to a wire-and-post gate next to a sign 'Monte Repoblado: Por Favor Cierren La Cancela'. Beyond the gate head straight along an indistinct path following cairns along the top of a ridge. After 80m the path cuts left, descends, then bears once more right as it drops down through pine trees and ferns. Crossing a plastic water pipe it angles left then reaches a flat stretch of rock. Here bear slightly left. Looping right then left the path crosses a streambed then runs just left of a fence. Follow the fence for 50m, climb down a low wall, cut right through a wire-and-post gate then turn right again down a concreted track.

You soon reach the first houses of **El Pelayo** where, arcing left, the track runs up to a junction by a house signed 'La Alquería'. Here turn right and go down Calle Sierra de Lucena for 100m to a 'Stop' sign just before the N-340. Turn left and go along the road for 250m to reach **Restaurante las Piedras** and a pedestrian **bridge** spanning the N-340 (**7hr 5min**).

The Strait of Gibraltar comes into view and, beyond, the towering massif of Jebel Musa.

EL PELAYO (POPULATION 851, ALTITUDE 253M)

The small village of El Pelayo fans out to either side of the N-340 which connects Alegeciras and Cádiz. There's more to the village than you see at first glance: most of its houses are tucked down beneath the road. Northeast of the village lie the thickly wooded hillsides of La Sierra de Algarrobo while to the southwest its municipal borders run down to the Mediterranean from where there are views out across the Strait to the mountains of northern Morocco.

A village grew up here because of the abundant spring waters which well up at El Chorro de Pelayo: even in years of drought this source of artesian water has never dried up. Today El Pelayo has become a dormitory village to Algeciras which lies just seven kilometres to the south and where many more jobs are to be found.

This stretch of Andalucía's coast has long been a sensitive border area between North Africa and Europe as testified by the numerous *torres de vigilancia* (watchtowers) which were built to deter incursions of Mahgrebi corsairs in the 16th and 17th centuries: you pass one on Day 20.

The seaboard has once again become a sensitive spot on Spain's geo-political map since the advent of the *pateras* (open-topped boats) which over the past decades have attempted to smuggle sub-Saharan Africans across the Strait. Very few manage to give the Spanish coastal guards the slip now that a sophisticated satellite observation system has been set up, while a desperate adventure ends in tragedy for many when overloaded craft sink before reaching the Spanish coast.

Recommended accommodation

Huerta Grande €
www.huertagrande.com
Friendly eco-centre with accommodation in log cabins sleeping 2–6. To reach Huerta Grande, cross the bridge, turn right then go along the N-340 for 225m then turn left at a sign for 'Huerta Grande'. The hotel is 200m down the hill and is well signposted.

Recommended accommodation close to the village

Mesón de Sancho €€
www.mesondesancho.com
A few kilometres along the N-340 towards Tarifa, a comfortable roadside hotel and restaurant.

Or see Tarifa listings (Day 20).

Contacts

Ayuntamiento: www.algeciras.es
Taxi: in Algeciras Radio Taxi 956 606 060

DAY 20
El Pelayo to Tarifa

Start	The pedestrian bridge over the N-340, El Pelayo
Distance	17.4km
Ascent/Descent	165m/405m
Grade	Medium
Time	4hr 55min
Map	IGN 1:50000 Alegeciras 1078 & Tarifa 1077
Refreshments	None available en route

From the roadside hamlet of El Pelayo the Coast to Coast Walk leads on to Tarifa, the windy city whose fort and isthmus mark the boundary between the Atlantic Ocean and the Mediterranean sea.

After picking up a narrow footpath that cuts across a leafy copse just beneath the Huerta Grande log cabin complex you follow a broad dirt track for some 3km towards a high ridge topped by wind generators. Cutting left down a stony track you once again reach the waters of the Mediterranean which you left at the beginning of Day 1 of the Coast to Coast Walk.

Reaching the sea you head on along a beautiful path that weaves through the coastal scrub, a few metres in from the sea, which leads you to the tiny hamlet of Guadalmesí whose ancient watchtower protected the coastline from raids from North African corsairs.

From here you link in with the broad, coastal drovers' path which leads you on past several small coves where you could swim or break for a picnic.

The stage ends in Tarifa which you enter through the old town walls to reach the central square, La Plaza de Oviedo.

The stage begins next to the blue **pedestrian bridge** that spans the N-340 just south of **Restaurante las Piedras**. Cross to the west side of the bridge, turn right past Hostal El Jardín then head up the left side of the **N-340** then turn left at a sign 'Centro de Visitantes Huerta Grande'. Following a leafy tarmac road downhill you reach a metal gate and a fork. Here keep left following a sign

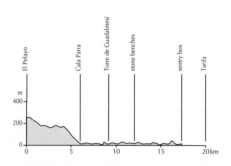

for 'Alojamiento Rural/Recepción'. Just as you reach a 10kmph speed limit sign cut left through a gate and follow a narrow path down to a streambed which you cross via stepping stones.

Beyond the stream the path runs close to the stream's left bank before it bears right and crosses back to the right bank via a second run of stepping stones beyond which it climbs to reach a fork. Take the right-hand branch then, reaching a second fork, once again bear right. After crossing another streambed you pass through a wire-and-post gate. Soon the sandy footpath reaches a metal gate. Beyond the gate, passing left of a farm shed, you reach a broad dirt track next to a pylon.

On a clear day Jebel Musa is visible on the other side of the Strait.

Turn left to follow the track then, reaching a second pylon, turn right and follow a sign 'Cortijo La Hoya' and 'Sendero Cerro del Tambor 4.5km'. The track angles round to the right as it crosses an open tract of land. ◄

THE PILLARS OF HERCULES

According to Greek then later Roman mythology the pillars marked the end of the westward extent of the travels of Hercules and upon which was written *Non Plus Ultra* meaning Nothing Lies Beyond. The Rock of Gibraltar was certainly the northern pillar while the location of the southern pillar is generally believed to have been either Jebel Musa in Morocco or Monte Hacho in Ceuta.

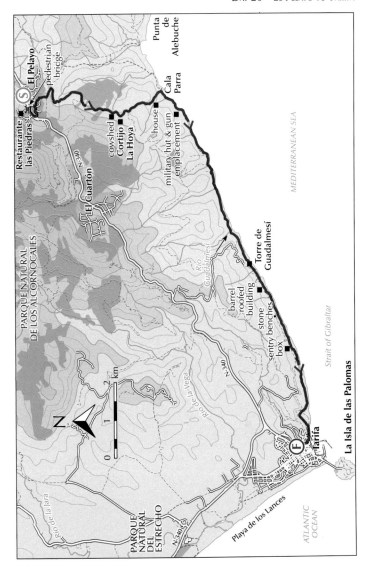

El Pelayo

Restaurante las Piedras

pedestrian bridge

Punta de Alebuche

Cala Parra

cowshed
Cortijo La Hoya

house

military hut & gun emplacement

El Cuartón

PARQUE NATURAL DE LOS ALCORNOCALES

N-340

Río Guadalmesí

Torre de Guadalmesí

barrel roofed building

stone sentry benches box

MEDITERRANEAN SEA

Strait of Gibraltar

Río de la Vega

N-340

Tarifa

La Isla de las Palomas

N-340

Río de la Jara

PARQUE NATURAL DEL ESTRECHO

N-340A/2

Playa de los Lances

ATLANTIC OCEAN

N

2 km

1

0

The coastline between El Pelayo and Tarifa

Soon the track arcs left, now running directly towards the ocean, then loops through a more wooded area. After crossing two cattle grids the track passes a barrel-roofed **cowshed** (55min).

You soon pass by the track which leads to **Cortijo La Hoya**. At 100m after passing a line of cypress trees the track angles hard right. Here turn left off the track down a narrow, stony track, heading straight towards the sea. The track passes left of a **house** with a green gate then narrows to become a footpath which threads through dense undergrowth. Some 100m before reaching the sea, where over to your left you'll spot a ruined building on a headland, the path divides. Here take the right-hand fork.

The path drops down to reach a wider footpath where, angling right for some 50m, you reach the Mediterranean and the beach of **Cala Parra**. After 75m the path, marked occasionally with yellow dots, angles up to the right and adopts a course parallel to the sea. After cutting back down to a more pebbly beach you reach a concrete bollard where the path again cuts inland. Passing between a **military hut** and a **gun emplacement** the path, occasionally braiding, passes through a metal gate. Some 30m beyond the gate you pass another ruined military building then descend to another stretch of pebbly beach. Continue along the beach for 50m then cut once more inland.

The path passes above a steep, eroded section of cliff where parallel strata of rock run out to the sea. Soon the Torre de Guadalmesí comes into sight. After crossing a streambed the path leads through a green metal gate then angles left and returns to the water's edge. After 75m angle right up a run of sandy steps then head on through a ramshackle gate made of an old bed base. After crossing more open ground you reach a fence where, passing through a stile and cutting left, the path widens then descends to a junction just inland from the Bay of Guadalmesí. Here cut left to reach the sea then follow a track which crosses the beach, fords the **Río Guadalmesí**, then loops steeply up to **La Torre de Guadalmesí (2hr 15min)**.

Beyond the tower continue along the broad track, parallel to the sea. Up ahead the lighthouse of Tarifa now comes into view on La Isla de las Palomas. The track crosses a cattle grid before passing a **barrel-roofed building** with blocked off windows. Stick to the main track which descends, crosses a concrete bridge spanning a stream before passing a sign 'Collado de la Costa y del Camino de Algeciras'. ▶

Shortly past the bridge the track swings up to the left as you reach another sign for 'Collado de la Costa' where, to your left, you'll see two **stone benches**. Here cut away from the main track to the benches. From here, maintaining your course parallel to the coast, you pass 30m above a stone building with a grey door at its eastern end. The indistinct path becomes more clearly defined while green V.P. posts help mark your way. A fence over to your right marks the boundary of a swathe of military-owned land.

The path occasionally braids: stick to the clearest path which leads you to a wire-and-post gate. Beyond the gate the path cuts through a rocky defile then runs

Green metal posts marked V.P. indicate the edges of the original drovers' track, the 'Collado de la Costa'.

A damaged
information board
tells of the mythology
of the creation of the
channel between
Europe and Africa
and the origins
of Jebel Musa.

parallel to the boundary fence of the military zone, which is to your right and which is also marked by low, white pyramids. Soon the path cuts away from the fence, still marked by green V.P. posts, then improves as it reaches a pole fence which you pass through via a V-shaped gap. Soon the footpath passes between a ruined military building with a rounded turret and ramshackle farm (**3hr 15min**). ◀

Heading past this building the lighthouse of Tarifa comes into view once again and, beyond it, your goal: the Atlantic Ocean. Green V.P. posts still mark your way, leading on round the upper reaches of a gully as you pass beneath a rectilinear villa, still just to the left of the rickety-posted fence. The path runs on to a second wooden railing where you pass through another V-shaped gap.

Beyond the gate follow the most obvious path across more shaly ground. Green V.P. markers guide you on past another modern house with a wind generator. After crossing a streambed the path angles right then passes behind a **sentry box**, then a subterranean military structure before it passes 50m to the right of an ugly, monolithic

*Sentry box looking
out to The Strait
and Morocco's
northern coastline*

building where there are a pair of benches. Running on across the hillside the path becomes clearer, occasionally running just outside the V.P. marker posts. Angling right it runs towards another wooden railing where heavy rain has washed part of the coastal hillside away. Above you are two white houses.

Here cut right through a gap in the fence, bear left above the landslide for 75m, then pass through a V-shaped gap in a rail-and-post fence for a third time. Continue along the footpath past two military pill boxes. ▶ The path becomes clearer as it angles away from the beach, crosses a wooden bridge (**4hr 25min**) then climbs two flights of wooden steps. At the top of the third flight, ignoring gates to your left and right, continue along a footpath which passes through another wooden railing via a V-shaped gap. The path angles through denser undergrowth then meets a track next to a sign for 'Parque Natural'.

Head straight across and continue along the narrow path which drops down through a thick stand of bamboo where it crosses a wooden bridge before reaching more

Sculptural century plants dot the hillside above the sea.

The ruined customs house at the entrance to Tarifa with Jebel Musa visible in the background

Tarifa's harbour now comes into view.

open terrain. Here stick to the higher footpath which runs past a small white building then descends to merge with a cobbled track. ◄ Reaching a junction bear right and continue along the cobbled track just to the right of the sea. You soon pass a marker post 'Tarifa-Guadalmesí 11.3 kms'. Bearing right the track reaches a junction.

Here cut left for 20m then bear right along Tarifa's old town wall following a sign for 'Ayuntamiento' then angle once again right to reach La Plazuela del Viento. Exit the square along Calle Aljaranda then take the second street to the right, Calle Coronel Moscardó. After passing the *correos* (post office) you reach the nerve centre of the old town, La Plaza de Oviedo, where the stage ends in front of the main entrance to San Mateo church (**4hr 55min**).

TARIFA (POPULATION 17,793, ALTITUDE 14M)

Statue of Sancho IV, commemorating the 500th anniversary of the Christian conquest of the town

Claimed by some sources to be the site of one of the mythical Pillars of Hercules, Tarifa lies to one side of the narrow isthmus of land where the Atlantic Ocean and Mediterranean Sea come together. Carthaginians and Phoenicians traded along this stretch of coast but it was not until the Roman period that a settlement known as Julia Traducta was founded here as a military outpost to the nearby town of Baelo Claudio.

The town takes its name from Tarif Ibn Malik who passed through in 710 when the first reconnaissance expedition of the Moors crossed the sea to Spain. Tarifa's fortifications date from the 10th century when the Caliphate in Córdoba feared a possible attack by the rival Fatami clan of North Africa. The town was conquered by the Christians after a six-month siege in 1292 while the following year Alonso Pérez de Gúzman repulsed an attempt to reconquer the fortress during which he sacrificed his 9-year-old son's life rather than surrender to the Moors. In so doing he earned his 'El Bueno' epithet. More heroics took place centuries later when an Anglo-Spanish army repulsed a Napoleonic force that outnumbered them three to one.

Fishing was always the town's main source of income until, some 25 years ago, Andalucía's Atlantic coast became one of Europe's chief meccas for wind and kite surfing. The arrival of a multi-ethnic surf community has transformed the town's fortunes and its narrow streets are now lined with shops, galleries and bars which exude a young, hip and friendly vibe. The town has a huge choice of accommodation and restaurants for all budgets: the recommendations here only scratch the surface.

The port of Tarifa serves as one of the main gateways to Morocco and North Africa with regular fast ferries ploughing to and fro to Tangier. It's also the point of departure for whale and dolphin spotting trips.

Your enjoyment of the city tends to be in direct relation to whether or not the Levante wind is blowing. While this desert wind from North Africa is the joy of the surfing community it can also whip up the sand and make Day 21 of the Coast to Coast Walk a greater challenge, even though you'll have the wind behind you. It's worth checking the forecast on Wind Guru (www.windguru.cz) before you set out.

Recommended accommodation
Posada Vagamundos €€
www.posadavagamundos.com
Characterful place within a 17th-century mansion house.

Hotel Misiana €€
www.misiana.com
At the heart of the old town with comfortable rooms. Those facing the street can be noisy.

La Estrella de Tarifa €€
www.laestrelladetarifa.com
Cosy hotel in the old town with Moroccan-inspired decor.

Hostal Gravina €€
www.gravina.es
Pristine rooms and apartments at the heart of the old town.

Contacts
Ayuntamiento: www.aytotarifa.com
Tourist Office: 956 680 993
Taxi: main rank 956 439 233

DAY 21

Tarifa to Bolonia

Start	La Plaza de Oviedo, Tarifa
Distance	20.5km
Ascent/Descent	40m/45m
Grade	Medium
Time	5hr
Map	IGN 1:50000 Tarifa 1077
Refreshments	Beach bars on Valdevaqueros beach

The final leg of the Coast to Coast Walk follows the ocean's edge nearly all the way from Tarifa to Bolonia. Leaving the old town by the causeway linking the old fortified town with El Castillo de Santa Catarina you first walk the length of the beach of Los Lances. This is one of the finest stretches of sand on Spain's Atlantic coast and when the wind is blowing you can expect to see hundreds of kite surfers cutting through the waves.

After rounding Punta de la Peña you head on across the bay of Valdevaqueros, still close to the water's edge. Leaving the bay the path winds between rocks then loops up to easier ground just above the sea as you pass round the second, smaller headland of Punta Paloma. From here the path runs past a series of smaller coves before reaching Bolonia's stunning arc of sandy beach.

The Coast to Coast Walk ends by a first aid hut at the edge of the village after 420km of trail.

These walking notes describe the best path to follow at high tide when you'll occasionally need to cut a few metres inland. At low tide you can stick to the ocean's edge nearly all of the way: it's largely a question of following your instincts.

Day 21 runs close to the ocean's edge with just a few ups and downs of less than 15m.

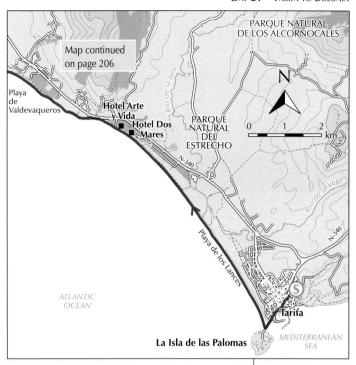

Map continued
on page 206

The stage begins in front of the main door of the San Mateo church at the centre of Tarifa's old town, to one side of the Plaza de Oviedo. With your back to the church head along Calle Sancho IV. The street bears left at Hotel Misiana, then right, then once more left. Following the road round to the right you pass El Castillo Gúzman el Bueno and a statue of Sancho IV El Bravo.

THE BRAVE AND THE GOOD

Sancho IV El Bravo or 'The Brave One' headed the Christian army that in 1292 reconquered Tarifa from the Moors. After a prolonged siege the city walls were broken down using rocks projected from huge catapults.

Gúzman el Bueno defended the city against a Moorish counter-attack two years later. Legend tells that the Moors had captured his younger son in an attempt to blackmail Gúzman into surrender. Gúzman supposedly threw a dagger over the town wall with which his son was sacrificed while refusing to surrender the town, thus earning his epithet El Bueno or 'The Good One'.

Heading straight past the entrance to the Estación Marítima continue along the causeway linking the old town and the fort of Santa Catarina. After passing a 'No Entry' sign cut right down to **Playa de los Lances** and head across to the ocean's edge where you meet the waters of the Atlantic for the first time.

The harder sand makes for much easier walking.

Head northwest along the ocean's edge. ◄ Leaving the town's sprawling western suburb behind, which is over to your right, you pass by a wooden lifeguard's hut. In the distance, to your right, you'll see one of the largest wind farms in Europe. Continuing along the beach you

Agave beside the coastal footpath between Tarifa and Bolonia

reach the riverbed of the **Río de la Jara** (**50min**) at which point you may need to remove your boots and socks and cross the river. ▸

Approaching the beach's far end you pass the terracotta-coloured buildings of **Hotel Dos Mares**, surrounded by Washingtonia palm trees, then the cobalt blue buildings of **Hotel Arte y Vida**. Continue past a graffiti-daubed military pill box to reach a small bar at the very edge of the ocean. Pass just beneath the bar by clambering over the rocks then angle up right to find a better path.

Soon you drop down to the sea once more and cross a small beach accessed via a flight of wooden steps. Approximately 30m beyond the steps cut right, away from the rocks, up a sandy path. After just 10m, before reaching a circular viewing platform, angle left and descend to the next cove. At its far end continue along an indistinct path which passes another pill box (**1hr 55min**) beyond which you reach **Playa de Valdevaqueros**. Walking northwest along the sand you pass the small lagoon formed at

If after very heavy rain the river looks impassable head further inland to cross the river by a bridge.

The beach beyond Valdevaqueros

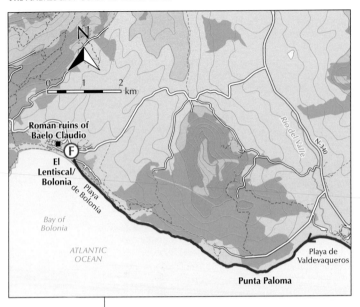

A small spring at the end of this stretch of sand is a popular spot for taking a cleansing mud bath.

the point where the **Río del Valle** runs up to meet the sea. At the far end of the beach angle right through a breach in the headland to reach the next beach. ◄

Continue to the beach's far end then pick your way across rocks then continue along the next stretch of sand. At high tide it's easier to angle right and follow a path that runs on through the dunes then shortly angles back down towards the beach as it passes beneath a pill box (**3hr**).

Continuing along the ocean's edge you round a low rocky headland (where you may need to remove your boots) then head along another stretch of sandy beach before traversing another headland. The path becomes clearer as it runs on, just left of a fence, then passes to the right of a large block of concrete, part of the abandoned coastal defences.

At a point where the path angles back down to the water's edge it's easier to stay high, following a path which runs just left of a fence. Threading through the undergrowth it passes above the next beach then runs on parallel to the sea. Passing above another stretch of beach the path angles once more back down to the sea where long strata of rock run parallel to the ocean's edge.

At the far end of this beach pick your way once more across the rocks then continue up a sandy path which cuts away from the sea. ▶ After running just above the beach the path cuts once more down to the sand where it passes another pill box (**4hr 25min**). Continue all the way to end of this section of beach. Threading your way between the rocks, then passing two more pill boxes, you reach **Playa de Bolonia**.

Continuing along the water's edge you pass the first beach bars of **Bolonia**. Reaching a wooden walkway that runs out towards the ocean's edge cut right and follow it inland past a shower to reach a yellow, wooden first aid hut and the end point of the Coast to Coast Walk (**5hr**).

Looking back you'll now see the Tarifa lighthouse on La Isla de las Palomas.

BOLONIA (ALSO KNOWN AS EL LENTISCAL) (POPULATION 330, ALTITUDE 5M)

The beach and the Roman ruins of Baelo Claudio, Bolonia

The bay of Bolonia describes a gentle arc between the hillside of San Bartolomé and the Sierra de la Plata. Its 3km-long beach of fine white sand is among the most beautiful of the Atlantic coast and throughout summer serves as a magnet for thousands of visitors from throughout Spain. Many take time out to climb the enormous dune, which is among the largest in Europe, at the beach's northwestern end.

The seasonal variation in the temperature of the sea, just four to five degrees, is surprisingly small and you'll see people swimming here all year round. Others come to take a curative mud bath: at the southern end of the beach there are springs next to a point where seams of crumbly, grey shale can be scraped from between the rocks.

Bolonia first saw settlement in the second century BC when a sizeable Roman town named Baelo Claudio developed around the *salazones* (a place where fish is salted) where garum (a fermented fish sauce) was manufactured. The fish paste was exported throughout the empire and was to make the municipality of Baelo Claudio among the richest in Iberia. The town took its name from the emperor Claudius who granted the settlement the title of town.

The Roman urbis (city) never recovered from the damage caused by a huge earthquake at the end of the third century AD and was to suffer constant attacks by North African pirates. By the time the Visigoths arrived in Spain in the 5th century the place lay in ruins. Baelo Claudio makes for a fascinating visit: a recently inaugurated museum contains state-of-the-art, interactive displays about the place's history. The building's minimalistic design and location gave rise to considerable controversy at the time of its construction.

During the winter months not a great deal happens in the village and many of the *chiringuitos* (beach bars set up for the summer season) and restaurants shut up for the season. Fish should be your first choice when it comes to eating out: there are a several excellent restaurants within yards of the end point of the Coast to Coast Walk.

Recommended accommodation

La Hormiga Voladora €€
www.lahormigavoladora.com
Hostel with garden next to the beach. Rooms and self-catering apartments.

Hostal Rios €€
www.hostalriosbolonia.com
Simple hostel with small en suite rooms and a restaurant.

Hostal Los Jerezanos €–€€
www.hostallosjerezanos.es
Friendly hostel with pool and first floor rooms with terraces with sea views.

Contacts

Ayuntamiento: www.aytotarifa.com
Taxi: nearest taxis in Tarifa, main rank 956 439 233

Baelo Claudio Archaeological Site
www.juntadeandalucia.es/cultura/museos/CABC/
Summer opening Mon–Sat 10am–2pm, 5pm–7pm, Sun 10am–2pm
Winter opening Mon–Sat 10am–2pm, 4pm–6pm, Sun 10am–2pm

APPENDIX A
Useful contacts

Many of the following websites are in Spanish by default, but most include the option of an English language version at the click of a button.

Transport

Train
Renfe (national rail operator)
(+34) 902 320 320
www.renfe.com

Buses

From Málaga and Seville
Autocares Los Amarillos
www.samar.es

From Jerez
Autocares Comes
www.tgcomes.es

Car Rental Agencies
All major car hire companies are present in Málaga and Seville and several also operate out of Jerez.

Maps
In Andalucía the best places to order maps are LTC in Seville (www.ltcideas. es/index.php/mapas) and Mapas y Compañia in Málaga (www.mapasy cia.es); in Madrid the best places are La Tienda Verde (www.tiendaverde.es) and Centro Nacional de Información Geográfica (www.cnig.es).

In the UK the best places for maps, which can be ordered online, are Stanfords (www.stanfords.co.uk) and The Map Shop (www.themapshop.co.uk).

Birdwatching and wildlife
The Andalucía Bird Society is a great first stop for anybody interested in the birdlife of the area (www.andaluciabird society.org).

Spanish Nature provide organised birding tours and walks in Andalucía and further afield. Contact Peter Jones via the website (www.spanishnature. com).

The Iberia Nature Forum provides comprehensive information, news and discussion about the plants and wildlife of the region (www.iberianatureforum. com).

Emergency services
Emergency services (general)112

Guardía Civil (police)
062

Local police
092

Medical emergencies
061

Fire service
080

British Consulate General (Madrid)
917 146 300

APPENDIX B
Glossary

Spanish	English
acequia	irrigation channel: many of those in Andalucía date from the Moorish period
alberca	water deposit
alcornoque	cork oak
alquería	from Arabic meaning 'a group of farm buildings'
arroyo	stream
ayuntamiento	town hall
barranco	ravine
boquete	pass or gap
calera	pit where lime was made by firing limestone
cañada	drovers' path or cart track
canuto	streambeds which have unusually diverse plant life, born of their moist, cloud forest-like climate
capilla	chapel
cerro	peak or mountain
collado	another term for drovers' path
cortijo	farm
coto (de caza)	hunting reserve
dehesa	forest which has been partially cleared to leave selected species
era	threshing floor
fuente	spring

APPENDIX B – GLOSSARY

Spanish	English
GR	abbreviation for Gran Recorrido or Long-Distance Footpath
ingenio	factory where sugar was manufactured from sugar cane
karst	type of deeply weathered limestone scenery
laja	jagged ridge formed when limestone strata run vertically upwards
mirador	viewing point
monte bajo	low-growing forest typical of parts of La Axarquía
mudéjar	referring to Moors who lived in Spain during the Reconquest
parador	state-owned hotel, often in a historic building
puente	bridge
puerto	mountain pass
sierra	mountain group
venta	roadside restaurant
vereda	footpath

APPENDIX C
Further reading

Recommended reading about travels on foot and horseback and by authors who have lived in the villages through which the walk passes.

David Baird, *East of Málaga*, Santana Books, 2008. A great general guide to just about every aspect of La Axarquía through which you pass during the first week of the walk.

David Baird, *Between Two Fires*, Maroma Press, 2011. How a guerrilla resistance group fought the Franco regime in the mountains near Frigiliana.

Alastair Boyd, *The Sierras of the South*, Santana Classics, 2004. A tender look at the villages of Andalucía, many of which you pass through on the Coast to Coast Walk.

Alastair Boyd, *The Road from Ronda*, Santana Classics, 2004. Boyd's earlier book about his forays on horseback from Ronda into the Andalucían mountains.

Penelope Chetwoode, *Two Middle-Aged Ladies in Andalusia*, John Murray Travel Classics, 2002. The eponymous middle-aged ladies were Chetwoode and her horse who together crossed a fair-sized slice of Andalucía.

Washington Irving, *Tales of the Alhambra*, Burlington Books, 2012. While much of the book is dedicated to the Alhambra it also contains fascinating narrative about Irving's journeys across Andalucía.

Laurie Lee, *As I Walked Out One Midsummer Morning*, Penguin Books, 2014. The richly evocative tale of Lee's journey on foot from Vigo to Andalucía, which coincided with the outbreak of the Spanish Civil War.

Botanical guides
Marjorie Blamey and Christopher Grey-Wilson, *Wildflowers of the Mediterranean*, A&C Black, 2004.

Davies and Gibbons, *A Field Guide to the Wild Flowers of Southern Europe*, The Crowood Press Ltd, 1993. A comprehensive work of manageable size.

Betty Molesworth Allen, *Wildflowers of Southern Spain*, Santana Books, 2000. A great local field guide although now difficult to find. Details medicinal/culinary uses of plants described and local folklore related to different species.

Oleg, Polunin and Smythies, *Flowers of Southwest Europe: A Field Guide*, Oxford University Press, 1998. Very comprehensive: the classic botanical must-have.

Ornithological guides
Peterson, Mountfort and Hollom, *A Field Guide to the Birds of Britain and Europe*, Houghton Mifflin Company, 2001.

Svensson, *Birds of Europe*, Princeton University Press, 2010.

Svensson, Mullarney and Zetterstom, *Collins Bird Guide*, Collins, 2010.

DOWNLOAD THE ROUTES
IN GPX FORMAT

All the routes in this guide are available for download from:

www.cicerone.co.uk/970/GPX

as GPX files. You should be able to load them into most formats of mobile device, whether GPS or smartphone.

When you go to this link, you will be asked for your email address and where you purchased the guide, and have the option to subscribe to the Cicerone e-newsletter.

www.cicerone.co.uk

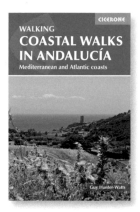
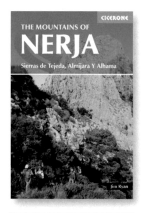
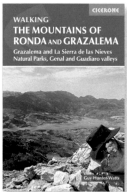
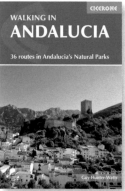

Walking – Trekking – Mountaineering – Climbing – Cycling

Over 40 years, Cicerone have built up an outstanding collection of over 300 guides, inspiring all sorts of amazing adventures.

 Every guide comes from extensive exploration and research by our expert authors, all with a passion for their subjects. They are frequently praised, endorsed and used by clubs, instructors and outdoor organisations.

All our titles can now be bought as **e-books**, **ePubs** and **Kindle** files and we also have an online magazine – **Cicerone Extra** – with features to help cyclists, climbers, walkers and trekkers choose their next adventure, at home or abroad.

Our website shows any **new information** we've had in since a book was published. Please do let us know if you find anything has changed, so that we can publish the latest details. On our **website** you'll also find great ideas and lots of detailed information about what's inside every guide and you can buy **individual routes** from many of them online.

It's easy to keep in touch with what's going on at Cicerone by getting our monthly **free e-newsletter**, which is full of offers, competitions, up-to-date information and topical articles. You can subscribe on our home page and also follow us on **Facebook** and **Twitter** or dip into our **blog**.

Cicerone – the very best guides for exploring the world.

CICERONE

Juniper House, Murley Moss, Oxenholme Road, Kendal, Cumbria LA9 7RL
Tel: 015395 62069 info@cicerone.co.uk
www.cicerone.co.uk